T0373787

For Mum, thank you for your never-ending support

URBAN HEALTHY RECIPES

AMS 2012

VEGGIE

VERY MUCH

DOT COM

Mirjam Leslie-Pringle

CLEARVIEW

Cover design: Mirnicology Studios, Nicolaas Homan
Cover photo: Mirjam Leslie-Pringle
Layout: Mirnicology Studios, Nicolaas Homan
Photography: Mirjam Leslie-Pringle
Photography pages 8, 12, 13, 16, 17 & 220: Jennifer Arndt

www.veggieverymuch.com

© 2016 Text and photos: Mirjam Leslie-Pringle
© 2016 First published in the Netherlands by Aerial Media Company bv, Tiel
© 2017 UK translation Clearview Books, London

First published in the UK in 2017 by Clearview Books,
22 Clarendon Gardens, London W9 1AZ

www.clearviewbooks.com

ISBN 978-1908337-436

All rights reserved. No part of this publication may be reproduced, stored in an electronic database or
published in any form whatsoever, be that by electronic or mechanical means, through photocopying or
audio/visual recordings, or in any other way without the express written permission of the publisher.

A CIP record of this book is available from the British Library

English translation: Danny Guinan, Wordforword
Editor: Jemima Dunne
Publisher: Catharine Snow
Production: Simonne Waud

Printed in Slovenia

CLEARVIEW

CONTENTS

INTRO

And then, all of a sudden, there it was – my *Veggie Very Much* cookbook.

One morning, just a few days after Christmas, I walked down the stairs to find that my husband had already opened the doors to let the sunlight stream into our old 'finca' on the island of Ibiza. I went into the kitchen to make myself an espresso – the way I always start my weekends. I sat down, turned on my computer and, still half asleep, waited for it to download my mail. After a quick check of my inbox, I opened a mail from someone who had addressed me very politely as 'Mrs Leslie Pringle'. At first I thought it was a promotional mail from a publisher recommending a new book but, as I continued, I realised that the mail was actually for and about me. It referred to my blog and the fact that I had already published two children's books and had co-worked on a number of other publications, but that I did not have my own cookbook yet. I felt something begin to tingle in my toes, a sensation that slowly began to spread up through my body. When I got to the bit asking me whether I would be interested to write my own cookbook, I must have jumped at least six feet into the air. YES! YES! was my hysterically happy response, though I still had absolutely no idea who the mail was from.

My husband walked in and asked me, in a slightly worried tone of voice (I don't want to say irritated because I was in fact behaving very strangely and was in danger of waking our kids who were still sound asleep upstairs) what was going on. I spent the next five minutes jumping up and down and exclaiming that this was the best belated Christmas present I could have wished for – my own cookbook. This was just what I had always wanted. A whole book full of delicious recipes and finger-licking photographs. I couldn't have been any happier.

Although our household wasn't strictly vegetarian when I was growing up, we never ate much meat. My brother, who is ten years older than me, left home when I was still in elementary school. And my father moved to the US when I was seven, so I did my growing up almost exclusively in the company of my mother. We lived in a forest and always had lots of animals around, which somehow always knew how to find us. The pitiful little animals needed our help and then ended up staying with us for the rest of their days. From dogs with bleeding paws to proud roosters without tails as well as starving hedgehogs to companionless chinchillas. Once a stray cow walked into our garden! Whatever animal happened to appear, we always preferred to see them alive and happy and free to roam our forest than dead and on our plates.

Very occasionally, my mother would cook a bit of minced meat or chicken, and rarer still there would be smoked sausage with mash. To be honest though, I preferred vegetables, potatoes and nice salads to a steak. I've never really had a craving for meat and later, when I started living on my own, this didn't change. I never bought meat myself, but if we went to visit people who did eat meat, I never made a song and dance about it.

As time went by my appetite for eating meat became less and less and then, when I got more and more into food, it disappeared altogether. I had never been very enthusiastic about fish (or shellfish) either, and

although many other vegetarians were hell-bent on telling me that fish suits a vegetarian diet very well, to me a fish is an animal and therefore not something I would wish to eat. Even though many of my friends ate very little meat, or none at all, I still experienced a lot of incomprehension from others. It has never been my intention to tell other people that they should become vegetarians or to say that eating meat is not right, but when people ask me for my opinion, I don't mind telling them why I believe it is healthier not to eat meat, or at least to eat a lot less of it. It is not only better for us, but it's also better for the environment and the poor animals that end their lives on our plates. I also found that there was very little for vegetarians to choose from in most restaurants, which I found to be rather bizarre given the endless possibilities offered by all the goodies that grow in the earth. There's a lot more to choose from than just goat's cheese salad or pizza Margeritha, although these can be very tasty too, of course.

I decided to put my ideas down on paper, which eventually resulted in my blog *VeggieVeryMuch.com* in 2012. I was soon having more and more fun thinking up, preparing and photographing new dishes using only vegetarian ingredients, and as a result I learnt

an awful lot about nutrition as well as how best to combine fruit, vegetables, grains, nuts and seeds. I got into the superfood hype for a while, and although I don't mind admitting that I would definitely take a bag of quinoa with me if I was banished to a desert island, I still think that the most important thing is to use your common sense when you are cooking and eating. Find out which vegetables are in season and what you need to eat to "feed" your body rather than just fill it up. Organic is better than sprayed – simply because there's less poison on or in the food. It is better to prepare your own dishes using fresh, unprocessed ingredients instead of opening a packet, because that way you consume fewer additives, such as sugars, emulsifiers, fillers, E-numbers and preservatives. And, of course, sourcing your vegetables and fruit from local farmers is better than buying stuff that is flown in from miles away, because: first, they're fresh and full of vitamins and secondly, they haven't had to make a long journey, hence less stress on the environment. All quite logical really. It is better to eat no or less meat, because the production of meat is the number one bad guy when it comes to the environment (check out this site if you're interested: www.cowspiracy.com) and red meat is being increasingly linked to all kinds of illnesses, including cancer and coronary disease. What about the

dairy industry, you might say? Well, not great either, if the truth be told, because the dairy industry causes just as much damage to the environment as the production of meat, and just as much, if not more, animal suffering. As my colleague, Wendy Walrabenstein, so eloquently puts it in her book *Food Body Mind*: "Treat meat and dairy products as delicacies, a gift from nature and not as a bulk product." I try to use dairy products as little as possible, and when I do I only use local organic products that come with a guarantee of optimum animal welfare.

The idea of writing a blog was not to try to convince people that they should eat less meat (or none at all), but more to inspire them by offering delicious and easy recipes using fresh and pure, seasonal ingredients that you can buy anywhere. That's why I call mine 'Urban Healthy Recipes' as they're tasty and healthy, the ingredients are easy to find and they're easy to prepare. I also found it important to demonstrate that vegetarian food is not boring or difficult to make. Many people cook their meals with meat simply because that's what they've been doing all their lives – the idea has literally been spoon-fed to them. But why would you want to continue eating meat every day when there are so many totally different possibilities on offer, ones that

are at least as tasty or even tastier? There are so many natural and fresh ingredients just screaming out to be used for, say, a complete Christmas dinner, a picnic on the beach, or a birthday party, without having to resort to meat at all, it's almost a no-brainer. And for all the veggies among us, I hoped my blog would offer lots of new recipes and ideas.

At the time, I was still living in Amsterdam with my husband and three children. We had a lovely house, which we hadn't quite finished renovating, but we continued to be drawn by the idea of moving abroad. We wanted to go and live in another country not just to to enjoy the sun and escape from the rat race, but also to be brave and bold enough to do it, instead of dreaming about endlessly. We also wanted to take the plunge before our eldest child was old enough to sabotage the idea. As a result one thing led to another and before we knew it we were planning a move to our beloved Ibiza. After a few scouting missions together with my husband, the whole family went to look at a few properties. We asked ourselves again whether we were really sure about it and the answer was a resounding 'yes'. Within four months we had moved to Ibiza, our island in the sun. We found an old finca, or farm cottage, with acres of space so that

even the horses – my first horse, which I had had since I was 13, a young horse we had saved from the slaughterhouse, and our little Shetland pony – could come too. We almost had our own riding stable. We squeezed everything we owned into one truck and off we went. It was the start of a wonderful adventure and not a day goes by now that I don't stop to think how grateful I am that we just threw caution to the wind and did it.

However, our first summer was quickly followed by our first winter, which took some getting used to. It was a very old house with thick walls, but no central heating, so it was far from comfortable. This really was 'back to basics'. We had to learn that it was important to get the wood stove going early in the morning and to put on an extra log each night before we went to bed to keep it in for the night. We also had to chop all our own wood. We even had to drive to the other side of the village to turn the central switch back on whenever the fuses blew. If we wanted to harvest a single tomato then the vegetable garden really needed to be watered *every day*; and that if you forgot something in the shop (9 miles away), it was just bad luck. We also learned how the seasons work here: which insects came and when; when the different plants grow and bear their fuit or veg; when I could expect the flowers to start appearing or see the blossoms appear on the almond tree; how the pomegranates grew and when the fig trees started to bud. We were right in the middle of it all and there was no escape.

There's a lot of work on our 'farm', but it felt great to drive home through the mountains and see the horses waiting for you outside the house and the dogs barking and running towards the car. It's a bit like 'Little house on the prairie', way up in the mountains, miles away from everyone and everything. Slowly, but surely, we started to find our feet. We got to know the locals and made new friends through school and our work. I became familiar with the markets, the little eco stalls on the roadside, and finding the best little shops, for which I often had to make a detour. It was totally different from Amsterdam, where I could find everything I needed within a radius of 500 yards of our home. But where there is a will there is a way. And my blog, which had been in hibernation due to the move, was revived and began to grow steadily in popularity again.

Two winters later I received the aforementioned e-mail, and after a very pleasant meeting back in freezing cold Holland with my (soon-to-be) publishers, Hans and Peter, everything began to accelerate – The *Veggie Very Much* book was really going to happen. And soon, because even though it was already January we decided to aim for a summer release date. When Hans and Peter asked if that would be possible, I bravely answered 'Of course!'. I had faced bigger problems in my life before, I figured, but it would be quite a challenge to come up with 80 new recipes in three months. Eighty recipes alongside my work as a photographer and looking after my three children, four horses, two dogs, a cat, the house and the vegetable garden, not to mention my husband. But I didn't bat an eyelid and I and returned to Ibiza brimming with optimism. My husband, who (in my opinion) is a very talented designer, would take care of the design of the book, which was a big plus, because I loved everything I had seen him design down through the years. While I busied myself with the recipes, the styling and the photography, he took responsibility for the overall look. I have to admit that deciding on the design for the cover was not an entirely smooth process, but after some tetchy bouts of bickering we finally managed to come up with the desired result!

I am very happy to have been given the opportunity to create this book, one in which I have been able to share not only the recipes themselves, but also the wonderful environment that allowed me to create them – the places, the situations, the leftovers in the fridge, and so on. None of it would have been possible without the help of the wonderfully creative people around me, who love good food as much as I do. The book has turned out exactly the way I wanted, and it is my fervent hope that it will inspire in you the same warm feeling as the one with which it was made.

Mirjam

Before we
GET STARTED...

The recipes in this book are easy to make. Some might need a little bit more attention than others, but in general anyone can make them. These days most of us find ourselves pressed for time, so preparing fresh food should not be too complicated and the ingredients need to be readily available. The latter is a must in my opinion: you shouldn't have to go to four different shops to get all ingredients you need and still end up missing something.

My husband, Nicholas, has been spending a lot more time in the kitchen than he was used to because I was too busy either writing or taking photos, but this turned out to be a good test case for the book. Armed with the rough recipes on his iPad, he set about preparing a lot of the dishes that would eventually make it into the book. And he got on so well that... well, if he can do it... you know what I mean!

I would also like to point out that I have not indicated whether all the ingredients are organic or not; you can assume that about 80 percent of what I use is organic or made using local seasonal products. So about 20 percent is not organic, simply because the organic option was unavailable or could not be found. I use very little dairy (milk or cream), but use eggs and cheese a bit more. And when I do buy these 'animal' products I always buy 100 percent organic and only after having been told exactly where they come from so that I am sure nothing has been done to impinge upon the animal's welfare.

I believe it is important to strive for the best quality where and whenever possible (for humans and for animals). But again: it should all be both practical and doable.

Now, give it your best shot, but be sure to enjoy yourself too. Tasty and healthy food should always be fun to make and eat!

Oven temperatures

°C	Fan °C	°F	Gas	Description
110	90	225	¼	Very cool
120	100	250	½	Very cool
140	120	275	1	Cool
150	130	300	2	Cool
160	140	325	3	Warm
180	160	350	4	Moderate
190	170	375	5	Moderately hot
200	180	400	6	Fairly hot
220	200	425	7	Hot
230	210	450	8	Very hot
240	220	475	8	Very hot

Weights for dry ingredients

Metric	Imperial	Metric	Imperial
7g	¼ oz	425g	15oz
15g	½ oz	450g	1lb
20g	¾ oz	500g	1lb 2oz
25g	1 oz	550g	1¼lb
40g	1½oz	600g	1lb 5oz
50g	2oz	650g	1lb 7oz
60g	2½oz	675g	1½lb
75g	3oz	700g	1lb 9oz
100g	3½oz	750g	1lb 11oz
125g	4oz	800g	1¾lb
140g	4½oz	900g	2lb
150g	5oz	1kg	2¼lb
165g	5½oz	1.1kg	2½lb
175g	6oz	1.25kg	2¾lb
200g	7oz	1.35kg	3lb
225g	8oz	1.5kg	3lb 6oz
250g	9oz	1.8kg	4lb
275g	10oz	2kg	4½lb
300g	11oz	2.25kg	5lb
350g	12oz	2.5kg	5½lb
375g	13oz	2.75kg	6lb
400g	14oz		

Liquid measures

Metric	Imperial	Aus	US
25ml	1fl oz		
50ml	2fl oz	¼ cup	¼ cup
75ml	3fl oz		
100ml	3½fl oz		
120ml	4fl oz	½ cup	½ cup
150ml	5fl oz		
175ml	6fl oz	¾ cup	¾ cup
200ml	7fl oz		
250ml	8fl oz	1 cup	1 cup
300ml	10fl oz/½ pint	½ pint	1¼ cups
360ml	12fl oz		
400ml	14fl oz		
450ml	15fl oz	2 cups	2 cups/1 pint
600ml	1 pint	1 pint	2½ cups
750ml	1¼ pints		
900ml	1½ pints		
1 litre	1¾ pints	1¾ pints	1 quart
1.2 litres	2 pints		
1.4 litres	2½ pints		
1.5 litres	2¾ pints		
1.7 litres	3 pints		
2 litres	3½ pints		
3 litres	5¼ pints		

IN THE

MORNING

START YOUR DAY THE HEALTHY WAY

Oeuf
COCOTTE
with parsley pesto

I just love the weekend. There's no running around like crazy from six o'clock in the morning, like I have to during the week. Instead there's plenty of time to stretch, throw open the doors and windows, let the cats out and let the sunshine in. On days like this I can take my time over making breakfast for the family. There's the aroma of freshly brewed coffee, a hot oven, freshly squeezed juice and oeuf cocotte on the table in mini casserole dishes – this is the ultimate breakfast and one that even gets my daughter out of bed. These mini casserole dishes are a terrific invention, I've made all kinds of stuff in them, from mini quiches to little apple tarts. They're an absolute must in the kitchen – you'll need one per person for this recipe.

serves *4* | preparation time *20* minutes

Oeuf cocotte
olive oil for greasing
16 cherry tomatoes
8 eggs (preferably organic)
4 tbsp cream cheese: organic soya variety or
    Philadelphia
4 tbsp parsley pesto, right
a few sprigs of thyme
sea salt and freshly ground black pepper

Parsley pesto
120 ml olive oil
40–50 g parsley (1 large bunch), finely chopped
40 g Parmesan cheese, grated
1 clove of garlic, finely chopped
½ tsp freshly ground black pepper
zest of 1 lemon

Preheat the oven to 200 °C. Mix all the ingredients for the pesto together and set aside. Grease each one of the casserole dishes with a teaspoon of olive oil. Halve the tomatoes, divide among the dishes and season with salt and pepper. Break 2 eggs into each dish. Season again with salt and pepper. Put 1 heaped tablespoon of cream cheese into each dish and do the same with the pesto. Place the mini casserole dishes in a large oven dish and pour in enough boiling water (so that they can cook 'au bain-marie'). Place carefully in the oven and give them a quick check after about 10 minutes as some ovens bake faster than others. The eggs will take 10–14 minutes to cook. Serve with a slice of (spelt) toast – bon appétit.

Salty strawberry
SHAKE
with basil

When I was 17 I went to live in Istanbul and worked there for a while as a model; they are partial to a 'long, tall blonde' in Turkey. Inevitably I got my first taste of Turkish food at the same time, and there are lots of simply superb vegetarian dishes. We drank a lot of 'ayran' – a salty, chilled yoghurt drink that was perfect on really hot days. It turned out that it was also very easy to make – full-fat (Turkish) yoghurt, water and salt, that's all there is to it. My version here, with strawberries and basil, may not strictly deserve to be called 'ayran', but it is delicious nonetheless.

serves *2* | preparation time *5* minutes

150 g strawberries
250 ml organic full fat yoghurt
100 ml water
½ tsp Himalayan salt or sea salt
1 handful basil leaves
juice of ½ lime

Combine all the ingredients in a blender or with a hand blender, then leave in the fridge for an hour until well chilled.

FRIED EGGS

with broad beans

I was never a big fan of broad beans, probably because their outer skin is so tough that I couldn't fathom why anyone would want to eat them. Of course, I had no idea just how fabulous the beans were after you removed that outer shell, and neither did my mother, come to think of it. It takes a little time and effort, I'll admit, but the result is more than worth it. Young, fresh broad beans are available in June and July, but you can always keep them in the freezer too. They are extremely tasty and terrific with yoghurt and fresh mint. This makes a superb breakfast if you have the time.

serves *2* | preparation time *5* minutes

150 g broad beans
4 or 5 eggs
1 tbsp olive oil for frying
1 handful fresh mint
4 heaped tbsp Greek yoghurt
sea salt and freshly ground black pepper
wholemeal toast (optional)

Bring a saucepan of water to the boil, add the broad beans and blanch for 1 or 2 minutes. Drain and set aside to cool. Using a sharp knife, cut an opening in the outer skin and pop out the bean; repeat to skin all the beans. Heat the olive oil in a frying pan, break the eggs straight into the pan, prick the yolks with a fork and leave to fry gently. After 2 minutes add the beans and fry until the egg whites are done and the yolks are to your liking. Remove from the heat, spoon in the yoghurt, season with salt and pepper and garnish with chopped mint. This is excellent with a slice of wholemeal toast.

In the Morning

Pure mango & strawberry
ICE CREAM

How would you like to be a teenager who gets to wake up in his best friend's house at whatever time of the day he likes and find himself being spoiled rotten by his 'surrogate mum' just because he is in town for a few days before he has to leave again to join his own family in Ibiza. My son really does have the best of both worlds. His number one amigo is the son of my best friend, Nanda, which means that a lot of travelling goes on between our respective addresses during the holidays. My son loves to go back to the Netherlands every so often to see his old friends, secure in the knowledge that he will be doted upon as much there as he is here at home – Nanda pulls out all the stops whenever he comes to visit. Each morning the two boys get to say what they would like for breakfast and nine times out of ten they plump for her freshly made mango and frozen strawberry ice cream sorbet. Lucky things!

serves *2* | preparation time *5* minutes

1 greenish mango, not too ripe (or all you'll get is mush)
250 g frozen strawberries

Take the strawberries out of the freezer and allow them to thaw for a little while a little before you peel and chop up the mango. Add the lot to a bowl and mix together using a hand blender. Serve immediately.

In the Morning

Griddled
ASPARAGUS WITH EGGS

and Parmesan cheese

Sometimes perfection can be ridiculously easy to achieve. When a friend of mine came to stay in our guesthouse for a few days, she told me about her 'Thai friend who was married to an Italian man who often made this breakfast for her when they lived in India'. While I was trying to figure out this conundrum, she started unpacking a bag full of groceries and proceeded to cook up a storm in the kitchen. It wasn't difficult to make, she promised me, and there would even be some left over for Nicholas. She was right about the first bit, but there was nothing left over.

serves *2* | preparation time *15* minutes

250 g asparagus (1 bunch)
1 tbsp olive oil
1 tbsp butter
4 or 5 eggs
sea salt and freshly ground black pepper
5 tbsp Parmesan cheese, grated

Wash the asparagus and chop off the ends – about 1½–2 cm. Heat the olive oil in a griddle pan and cook the asparagus for about 5 minutes; sprinkle with a little salt and pepper. Heat the butter in a frying pan, add the asparagus and then the eggs (without breaking the yolks), add another sprinkling of salt and pepper, cover with a lid and leave to cook on a low heat until the eggs are done – from 5 to 7 minutes, depending on how hard you like your eggs. Sprinkle the grated Parmesan cheese over the top and serve.

OVERNIGHT OATS

with golden milk

———

Golden milk is an ancient Ayurvedic drink whose most important ingredient is turmeric. The principal constituent of turmeric is curcumin, which is similar to ginger in taste. Curcumin has very effective purification and anti-inflammatory properties and is full of antioxidants. The list of beneficial qualities goes on and on. Turmeric is very popular in Indian cooking and is the basic ingredient in many curries. The flavour of turmeric becomes even more potent when it is dissolved in fat together with black pepper, which explains the addition of a teaspoon of coconut oil in my recipe, but you can also use olive oil or linseed oil if you wish.

I often drink a cup of golden milk at night; it is soothingly warm and tasty. Then one day it occurred to me that it might also go very well with porridge oats and be a great source of nutrients at the start of the day, too. If you get everything ready the night before and leave the oats to steep in the fridge, your breakfast will be ready in no time in the morning. Steeping the oats is important as it reduces the amount of phytic acid, which is an 'anti-nutrient' that thwarts the body's efforts to extract nutrients from food. The oats can be eaten cold, straight from the fridge, but I prefer to heat them, and the apples, for a few minutes before tucking in.

serves *1* | preparation time *10* minutes (plus 1 night in the fridge)

½ tsp turmeric
1 tsp cinnamon
½ tsp ginger
freshly ground black pepper
200 ml almond milk
½ apple

30 g whole oats
10 almonds, crushed
1 tsp coconut oil
a little (raw) honey to taste
½ banana, sliced

First, mix the turmeric, cinnamon, ginger and pepper together with a few teaspoons of almond milk until you have a smooth paste; this will prevent lumps from forming later on. Peel the apple, chop into small slices and add to a bowl, together with the almond milk, oatmeal, almonds, turmeric mixture and the coconut oil. Cover tightly with cling film and leave to steep in the fridge for at least 8 hours. In the morning, bring the mixture briefly to the boil. Add a little honey if you wish (but never cook the honey) and a few slices of banana. There's no better way to start the day.

In the Morning

CHACHI

Okay, the name is a bit odd, I'll admit, and I have Googled it, asked the regulars in the local café here in Sant Juan and even quizzed the French lady who works in the bakery – why 'chachi'? No one could enlighten me. It sounds more like Chinese than Spanish to be honest, but I can't find an explanation for the name anywhere. In any event, it is absolutely delicious and 100 percent Spanish, that much I know. The trick lies in what you choose to hide under the eggs.

The Spanish have a habit of rubbing tomato seeds and garlic into their toast and panini bread. The result is quite delicious, but I've changed the recipe a little here because I don't always like having the strong taste of garlic in my mouth – this version is no less tasty though.

serves *2* | preparation time *10* minutes

1 tomato
2 tbsp olive oil
2 eggs
2 slices of good-quality wholemeal or sourdough bread
sea salt and freshly ground black pepper
1 avocado, peeled and sliced
2 slices of cheese

Bring a saucepan of water to the boil, score the skin of the tomato and cook it for 1 minute – this makes it easier to remove the skin. Heat 1 tablespoon of olive oil in a frying pan and fry the eggs sunny side up until almost done. Remove the eggs from the frying pan and set aside on a plate. Turn down the heat and place the slices of bread in the frying pan. Use a hand blender to mix the tomato with the other tablespoon of olive oil, pepper and salt. Spread this mix on the slices of bread. Place the avocado on top, followed by the cheese and the fried eggs. Cover with a lid and leave on a low heat until the cheese has melted. Season with salt and pepper and dig in! Serve any leftover avocado on the side.

In the Morning

American
BLUEBERRY
pancakes, the ultimate recipe

Just because something is delicious it doesn't mean it has to be a disaster for your waistline. You can make these all-American pancakes so that they are actually good for you by using oat flour instead of ordinary white flour. Oats are gluten-free, have a low glycemic index and are a terrific and long-lasting source of energy. This is a clever way of getting your kids to eat a nourishing breakfast without them realising it.

for *12* pancakes | preparation time *35* minutes

Oatmeal pancakes
250 g oat flour
1 egg
1 tsp baking powder
350 ml oat milk or almond milk
1 banana
½ tsp salt
butter for frying

Blueberry sauce
250 g blueberries
2 tbsp agave syrup
1 tbsp lemon juice
flesh of 1 vanilla pod

You can buy oat flour, but it is also very easy to make it yourself. Just grind some oats in a food processor or with a hand blender until you have a fine flour. Mix the oat flour with the egg, baking powder, milk, banana and salt until you have a smooth batter. Heat a knob of butter on a high heat in a frying pan and add enough of the batter so that you have a pancake about 10 cm in diameter. Turn down the heat a little and fry the pancake until you see small bubbles appearing. Flip it over and cook the other side until it is a nice golden brown too. Repeat until you have 12 pancakes. To make the sauce, mix the blueberries with the agave syrup and heat in a small saucepan. Cook on a low heat for 5 minutes, stirring continuously, until you have a nice smooth sauce. Then add the lemon juice and the vanilla and mix with your hand blender until completely smooth. Serve the pancakes in stacks of three, drizzle with the sauce and add a few thin slices of banana if you like.

Savoury
BROCCOLI MUFFINS

I am always looking for new ways to pack as much nutritious stuff as possible into tempting and tasty recipes. I do this mostly for the sake of my children, because although my mouth usually waters at the prospect of a vegetable such as broccoli, they are more inclined to turn their noses up in disgust. This can be frustrating at times, but I take great comfort in the belief that this is just another phase in their development and that they will overcome their aversion sooner or later. Until then I will continue to come up with whatever tricks I can to get them to eat their vegetables – and successfully I might add.

for *6* muffins | preparation time *40* minutes

150 g broccoli (florets and stem), sliced
6 eggs
100 g mature cheese, grated
1 tbsp dried thyme
50 ml (soya) cream

1 small clove of garlic, finely chopped
1 level tsp salt and freshly ground black pepper
12 (mixed) cherry tomatoes
Extra equipment: 6-section muffin tin and baking paper

Preheat the oven to 180 °C. Steam the broccoli for 5–7 minutes until done. In the meantime, mix the eggs, the grated cheese, thyme, cream, garlic, salt and pepper in a bowl with a hand blender until smooth. Then stir in the pieces of broccoli. Fill each section of the muffin tin with baking paper and pour in the broccoli mix until about three quarters full. Halve the cherry tomatoes and divide among the baking cases. Put the cases in the oven and bake the muffins for 25–30 minutes. Check them every now and then and turn your oven down if they are turning brown too quickly. The muffins are done when you prick one with a cocktail stick and it comes out dry. Remove the muffins, baking paper and all, from the muffin tin and leave to cool for 5 minutes before removing the baking paper.

In the Morning

Greek
YOGHURT
with griddled nectarines and pistachio nuts

This is dish is so fabulous that I have had to bump it up from the dessert menu to the breakfast table. The combination of Greek yoghurt and the sweetness of both the fruit and the maple syrup is divine enough, but the fact that the nectarines are roasted in lime juice before being served piping hot makes the whole package even more exciting.

serves *2* | preparation time *10* minutes

2 nectarines
2 tsp olive oil
1 lime, juice and zest
400 ml Greek yoghurt (approx.)
1 handful pistachio nuts
a few mint leaves for garnishing
2 tbsp maple syrup

Cut the nectarines in half, remove the seed and slice into chunks. Heat the olive oil in a griddle pan and cook the nectarine slices for about 2 minutes on each side. Then drizzle 2 tablespoons of lime juice over them. Spoon the yoghurt into two bowls and shell the pistachio nuts. Crush the nuts lightly and chop up the mint. Divide the nectarine slices between the bowls of yoghurt. Sprinkle with the pistachio nuts, drizzle with maple syrup and garnish with the mint and lime zest.

Quinoa-stuffed
OMELETTE

As I have already mentioned, quinoa is probably my favourite cooking ingredient. I find it not only delicious, but it is also a fantastic addition to the vegetarian diet. Quinoa contains more or less the same amount of proteins as eggs or meat – it contains all eight of the most essential amino acids that we need to ensure that we get enough protein into our bodies. Although it is usually eaten as a grain, quinoa is in fact a seed of South American origin. Quinoa can be eaten at any time of day, and combined with almost everything, from sweet to savoury dishes and from breakfast to salads or snacks.

for *1* omelette | preparation time *25* minutes

½ cup quinoa
8 cherry tomatoes
1 small handful fresh basil
1 small handful fresh coriander
½ avocado
1 tbsp extra virgin olive oil for the quinoa

Sea salt and freshly ground black pepper
2 eggs
2 tbsp unsweetened soya milk
2 tbsp olive oil for frying
chilli flakes, optional

Start by cooking the quinoa. For the perfect result, wash the quinoa under a fast-flowing tap, then cook it using 1 part quinoa to 2 parts water. Add a little salt to the pan and simmer for 12–14 minutes on a low heat with the lid on the saucepan. Cook until the white spots in the middle of the grains have disappeared. If necessary, drain off any excess water and set the quinoa aside, covered. Cut the tomatoes in half, finely chop the fresh herbs and slice the avocado. Mix everything with 4 tablespoons of quinoa, the extra virgin olive oil, and a little salt and pepper. You can keep any leftover quinoa in a sealed container in the fridge. Beat the eggs with the milk, ¼ teaspoon of salt and a twist of pepper. Heat 2 teaspoons of olive oil in a frying pan, gently pour in the egg mix and fry the omelette on both sides on a medium heat until done. Transfer the omelette to a plate, spoon the quinoa salad onto one half of the omelette and fold over. Sprinkle with chilli flakes if you like.

Carrot love
100 ml carrot juice
100 ml fresh orange juice
Juice of ½ lemon
1 apple

Apple de luxe
2 apples, peeled
½ cucumber, peeled
5 leaves of basil
juice of ½ lemon
150 ml water

Delicious oats
150 ml yoghurt
2 tbsp oatmeal
50 ml almond milk
1 banana
a pinch of cinnamon
1 mango

SMOOTHIES

with and without yoghurt

Weekday mornings in our house are a little chaotic, to say the least. I often wonder how other families manage with three children who all need to be in different places at the same time. The alarm clock goes off at 6.15 a.m. and, even after hitting the snooze button a few times, I am still always the first one up. There are school lunches to be made, children to be woken (again and again) and then taken to school – preferably with something in their stomachs. Getting kids to eat something before going to school is a struggle at the best of times but smoothies invariably do the job. They're extremely handy, ready in no time at all, and can even be gulped down in the car if needs be. Pile everything into the blender, a quick whizz and you've got a breakfast bursting with fibre and vitamins.

serves *1-2* | preparation time *5-10* minutes

Put all the ingredients in the blender mix until you have a nice, creamy smoothie.

Sexy berries
150 g raspberries
150 g blueberries
1 pear
150 ml almond or soya milk
10 mint leaves

Friendship orange
200 ml orange juice
5 strawberries
1 banana
1 kiwi
10 mint leaves

HASHBROWNS

with courgette and sweet potato

When I was young I went to visit family in Australia a few times with my mother and we always ended up going on fantastic trips that my uncle would plan meticulously in advance of our arrival. We drove all around Australia and the long journeys usually meant having to get up every day at around 6 a.m. Breakfast always consisted of hashbrowns, and how I loved them – they're like compact pancakes of potato and onion. Later on, I experimented with the recipe using all kinds of different ingredients. This variation is simply delicious, and there's not a potato in sight.

serves *3-4* | preparation time *25* minutes

2 medium-sized courgettes
1 medium-sized sweet potato
1 tsp sea salt
40 g Parmesan cheese, grated
1 handful flat leaf parsley, finely chopped

2 cloves of garlic
1 egg
sea salt and freshly ground black pepper
1 tsp cumin
2 tbsp olive oil

Grate the courgettes and the peeled sweet potato roughly and mix with 1 teaspoon of sea salt. Place in a colander and set aside for 10 minutes to draw out the moisture. Then use kitchen paper or a clean teacloth to dry off any remaining drops of moisture. Place the courgette and sweet potato in a large bowl and mix in the Parmesan cheese, parsley, crushed garlic and the egg. Season with salt, pepper and cumin. Heat the olive oil in a large frying pan and using a tablespoon, add in the mix, flattening it down as you do so. Your hashbrowns should be about 7 cm in diameter and 1 cm thick. Fry them until golden brown on one side and then flip over. Fry for another 4 to 5 minutes on both sides on a low to medium heat.

In the Morning

Homemade
GRANOLA

If you like yoghurt and muesli, then homemade granola is an absolute must. You can make as much as you like and store it in a sealed jar. It makes a great breakfast in the morning, but is just as delicious at any other time of the day. The basic ingredients are oats and nuts, but you can be as adventurous as you like.

for *1* kg | preparation time *60* minutes

white of 1 egg
250 g oatmeal
250 g mixed unroasted nuts, crushed (for example, almonds, walnuts, pistachio nuts, pecan nuts, macadamia nuts)
120 ml maple syrup
60 ml liquid coconut oil (melted in a saucepan)
50 g sesame seeds
1½ tsp sea salt
2 tsp cinnamon

50 g sunflower seeds
50 g pumpkin seeds
50 g raisins
50 g cranberries
150 g coconut chips (or dried coconut)

Preheat the oven to 150 °C. Beat the egg white and mix it with all the other ingredients, except for the raisins, cranberries and coconut chips. Spread the granola out on a baking tray covered with baking paper and bake for about 30 minutes until crispy and golden brown. Give the granola a stir every 10 minutes to prevent it from burning. Remove from the oven and mix in the raisins, cranberries and coconut chips when the granola has cooled sufficiently. It can be stored for up to two weeks in a well-sealed jar. Granola is great served with organic yoghurt and fresh figs or blueberries.

IN THE

AFTERNOON

LIGHT AND DELIGHTFUL

BURRATA SALAD

with beans and fresh herbs

The first time I ate a burrata salad I almost gasped in amazement at the softness of the fresh cheese! I first had it on Ibiza, in a fabulous little restaurant known only to insiders and almost impossible to find. The restaurant lies hidden in a tiny bay behind a mountain, which you first have to climb before descending along a narrow mountain path to a little, white wooden chiringuito with a huge fig tree growing on the beach outside the front door. The burrata appeared as a magnificent large ball of cheese covered in black salt, and it was so soft I could hardly believe it. I have refused to buy 'normal' mozzarella ever since – why choose the ordinary when you can have the very best.

serves *4* | preparation time *15* minutes

300 g French beans
400 g Spanish white beans (1 jar/tin)
2 avocados
2 handfuls fresh basil
2 handfuls fresh coriander
1 lemon, the zest and half of the juice

2 large balls of burrata or 4 small ones
2 tbsp capers
60 ml extra virgin olive oil
Himalayan or sea salt and freshly ground black pepper
1 block Parmesan cheese

Wash the French beans, trim the ends and cook the them for 4–5 minutes in a small saucepan with lightly salted water. Drain and transfer to a bowl of ice-cold water so that they keep their lovely green colour. After a few minutes drain again and dry with a tea towel. Rinse the Spanish white beans in a colander and pat dry. Peel and slice the avocados. Pluck the leaves from the basil and the coriander and set aside. Grate the skin of the lemon and then squeeze out the juice of one half. Place one small or half a large ball of burrata on each plate. Divide the beans, avocado, capers and herbs between the plates. Then sprinkle the lemon zest, olive oil and lemon juice over each one. Season with salt and pepper and top off with lashings of Parmesan cheese shavings.

In the afternoon

Warm
SALAD
with steamed broccoli and feta

One of the best things about living in Ibiza is the regular get-togethers that are organised 'en masse' within our group of friends (which is anything but your average bunch of Spanish amigos). Picnics on the beach are one of the ways in which we like to while away our Sundays together. The kids get to run around in their bare feet on the sand until the sun goes down, while the adults take the chance to catch up with each other before the week starts anew and everyone is busy with school and work again. We all bring something homemade – I'm usually in charge of the salads, while my English friends go all out with their Sunday roast. To each his own, of course – I tend to keep my distance from the carvery section. After all, I am the designated veggie and therefore responsible for getting enough greens and vitamins into everyone, and I don't mind my role one bit. Indeed, I raise a glass to it whenever I get the chance – cheers!

serves *6* | preparation time *20* minutes

200 g red quinoa
2 heads of broccoli
250 g cherry tomatoes
150 g block of feta
50 g walnuts

1 handful flat leaf parsley
60 ml extra virgin olive oil
juice of ½ lemon
sea salt and freshly ground black pepper
Extra equipment: a steam basket

Wash the quinoa then cook it, one part quinoa to two parts water and a pinch of salt, for 12–14 minutes. Drain, cover and leave to cool. Chop up the broccoli into small florets. Bring a saucepan of water (into which the steam basket fits perfectly) with a teaspoon of salt to the boil and steam the broccoli for 7 minutes – you may have to do this in batches, depending on the size of your steamer. In the meantime, halve the tomatoes and slice the feta into small pieces. Crush the walnuts and finely chop the parsley. Mix everything into the quinoa, add the olive oil and lemon juice, then season with salt and pepper.

In the afternoon

Bumper
VEGETABLE TART

This mighty tart, or flan, is perfect for when you need to feed a lot of people at once. It is full of green vegetables and is a veritable explosion of taste. I often take one whenever we are going off on a trip, because it is just as good when eaten cold. You can serve it in smaller portions as a snack or for a picnic, or in larger portions for lunch.

serves *6-8* | preparation time *80* minutes

1 large white onion
1 large clove of garlic or 2 small ones
3 tbsp olive oil
150 g spinach
150 g broccoli
6 eggs
225 g tub of ricotta
100 ml (soya) cream
150 g mature cheese, grated

1 tbsp fresh or dried thyme, plus extra sprigs for garnishing
1 large roll of shortcrust pastry
100 g (frozen) peas
1 handful of basil
100 g gorgonzola or other blue cheese
sea salt and freshly ground black pepper
Extra equipment: 24 cm baking tin, baking paper

Preheat the oven to 180°C. Halve the onion and slice into thin rings. Finely chop the garlic. Heat the olive oil in a frying pan and fry the onion for 5–7 minutes until soft and golden brown. Add the garlic and fry for a few more minutes before adding the spinach. Cook the spinach until it has shrunk. Season with salt and pepper and set aside. Wash the broccoli, chop into small florets and set aside. Mix the eggs, ricotta, cream, grated cheese, (dried) thyme, 1 teaspoon of salt and a little pepper together until smooth. Chop up the basil, crumble the blue cheese and set aside. Line the baking tin with baking paper and then add the pastry; cut off any excess pastry around the edge. Start filling the pie by first adding a layer of the egg mix (about one third), then add half of the broccoli, half of the spinach and onion and half of the peas. Top this layer off with all of the basil and half of the blue cheese. Start again with the egg mix (one third), repeat the rest of the process as described above and finish off with the last of the egg mix and the blue cheese. Top off with a few sprigs of thyme and bake in the oven for 50 minutes. Check it every now and then and if you think the pie is baking too fast, turn the oven down a little. The tart is done when you prick it in the centre with a cocktail stick and it comes out (fairly) dry. Set aside to cool a little before serving while still hot, or leave to cool completely.

In the afternoon

Aunty Marcel's
STRAWBERRIES

We first met Marcel at a very weird quiz night that friends of ours had organised. It was a real hotchpotch of Germans, Dutch and English all mixed up together, and if I remember correctly, we even won the quiz. Marcel is Dutch, but had spent most of his life in Australia before moving to Ibiza – so a bit of a hotchpotch himself actually. We started chatting and the conversation eventually turned to children. He said he had already passed the age of 50 and had therefore probably missed the boat as far as children are concerned. Despite my protestations he insisted that he really didn't mind. His friends have plenty of children and he always seems to end up in the kitchen cooking for them; not surprising really, given that he is a chef by profession and everyone just adores his cooking – which has a heavy vegetarian slant – he is obviously the caring type. Curiously enough, the kids all call him 'Aunty Marcel' – don't ask me why. He first introduced us to this strawberry salad one day when we were having lunch on the beach. Since that day I firmly believe that this is the only way to eat strawberries, and preferably out of a huge big bowl.

serves *4-6* | preparation time *15* minutes

500 g strawberries, quartered
2 limes, juice and zest
2 handfuls fresh basil, finely chopped
2 handfuls fresh coriander, finely chopped
4 tbsp extra virgin olive oil
sea salt and freshly ground black pepper

Mix everything together, season with salt and pepper, and leave for half an hour before serving.

In the afternoon

Spicy
CHICKPEA SALAD

Beans, in all shapes and sizes, feature high on my list of favourite foods, and the number one bean must surely be chickpeas. They're not only delicious in a wide variety of dishes (hummus, salads, soups, and so on), but also very good for you. For vegetarians especially, chickpeas are an excellent substitute for meat, and they're a great alternative to eggs for vegans. Chickpeas are packed with essential vitamins, like B_{12}, that are mainly found in animal products. They contain iron, vitamins C and B_6 and folic acid: all very important minerals and vitamins. All in all eating chickpeas is a great idea. In this salad the chickpeas are roasted slowly in chilli powder, which makes them deliciously spicy and crunchy. Our friend Evert-Jan once said to me: "Mirjam, if everything should ever go completely wrong when I am making dinner, then at least I know I can always fall back on your spicy chickpea salad.".

serves *4* | preparation time *15* minutes

Chickpea salad
400 g chickpeas (from a jar/tin), drained
2 tbsp olive oil for frying
1 tsp chilli powder
1 tsp sea salt
250 g cherry tomatoes or small roma tomatoes
1 cucumber
3 spring onions
1 red onion
50 g black olives, deseeded

2 large handfuls parsley
1 handful fresh mint leaves

Dressing
60 ml extra virgin olive oil
4 tsp white balsamic vinegar
juice of 1 small lemon
1 tsp sea salt
freshly ground black pepper

Heat the olive oil in a frying pan, then add the chickpeas, chilli powder and salt. Stir together over a medium heat – if the chickpeas start 'jumping' in the frying pan, turn the heat down a little. Fry for 10 minutes, stirring occasionally. Cut the tomatoes into quarters. Peel the cucumber and chop into small pieces. Chop the spring onions into thin rings and dice the red onion. Slice the olives, remove the stalks from the parsley and chop up the mint roughly. Mix together everything except the chickpeas in a salad bowl. Make the dressing by putting all of the ingredients into a jar, closing the lid firmly and giving the whole lot a good shake. Pour the dressing over the salad and then add the chickpeas. Season to taste with sea salt and freshly ground black pepper.

In the afternoon

LENTIL SALAD

with raw courgette

This salad is loosely based on one I once had at a birthday party. One of my friend's son had turned four, but I believe I spent longer staring at the bowl of lentils than at the splendid birthday cake that was trotted out at the end of the day. I was so enthralled by the sight of the salad that when I got home that evening I went straight to the kitchen and set about making it myself. I tell my friends, Maartje and Ruben, that I have no idea if it bears any resemblance to their creation, but it tastes really good.

serves *4-6* | preparation time *15* minutes

200 g dried brown lentils
3 bay leaves
2 cloves of garlic
½ red onion
½ courgette
2 handfuls flat leaf parsley, finely chopped

1 handful small gherkins, sliced
60 ml extra virgin olive oil
1 lime, juice and zest
2 tsp sea salt
freshly ground black pepper

Wash the lentils and cook them in plenty of water with the bay leaves and the garlic for about 18 minutes until done (don't let them get too soft and don't add any salt to the water, otherwise they will start to break up). Drain and remove the bay leaves and garlic. Set aside while you attend to the rest. Chop the onion very finely and then the courgette into very small cubes. Mix both together with the parsley and the gherkin. Add the olive oil, the zest and the juice of the lime and finally the lentils. Give it a good stir and season to taste with sea salt and a little pepper.

In the afternoon

Buckwheat and chickpea flour
PANCAKES

I can still see Nan (my 'bestie' with her fabulous red curls) standing at my front door with a stack of buckwheat and chickpea flour pancakes. At first I wasn't sure what to think, worried that Nan had suddenly gone all sandals and white socks on me. But the girl wasn't for turning and she insisted that I taste them. She said that they were the most wonderfully delicious and healthy pancakes, that you could put anything on them, and that they were the perfect accompaniment for an aperitif. Plus they're a lot better for you than the bags of crisps we were used to demolishing during our frequent chats. Okay, okay, I gave in – at least she wasn't threatening me with being teetotal as well. We made some hummus to go with the pancakes, and quickly found out that olive tapenade and soft goat's cheese were great on them too. I haven't looked back.

serves *4* | preparation time *30* minutes (for 16 pancakes)

125 g buckwheat
125 g chickpea flour
100 ml olive oil
650 ml water
¼ tsp salt
olive oil for frying

Mix all the ingredients together thoroughly with your hand blender. Then fry the pancakes in a small frying pan with a teaspoon of olive oil. They are great with any type of tapenade, goat's cheese, guacamole and hummus.

In the afternoon

Salad of curly endive and
CANNELLINI BEANS
with cauliflower 'rice'

It was a balmy summer evening in Amsterdam and Nicholas and I were going out for dinner. We had hired a babysitter on the spur of the moment, hopped on our bikes and headed off into the night. Incidentally, we brought those same bicycles with us to Ibiza, but they were never much use other than as a reminder of lovely Amsterdam after we found out that cycling five miles up and down a mountain for a baguette and a cup of coffee was not really the clever thing to do on this island. But back to the evening in question. We found ourselves sitting in a fabulous Italian restaurant, whose name I cannot remember, but it was one we frequented many times thereafter. It was an evening of great wine and great food. It was the first time I discovered this salad of endive, cannellini beans and rosemary, which it proved to be the perfect start to a marvellous night. Now cauliflower rice might sound a little – well, how should I put it – macrobiotic to most people, I know, but don't let the name put you off. Cauliflower is great in all kinds of dishes and given that we already eat cauliflower 'steak', cauliflower pizza and even cauliflower lollipops, I think we can safely add cauliflower rice to the list.

serves *4* | preparation time *30* minutes

Salad
½ cauliflower
2 tbsp olive oil for frying
1 clove of garlic, crushed
1 tbsp dried rosemary
sea salt and freshly ground black pepper
150 g curly endive
400 g cannellini beans (from a jar/tin), drained

Dressing
60 ml olive oil
2 tbsp dried rosemary
½ tsp sea salt and freshly ground black pepper

Chop the cauliflower into chunks (use the stem too, it's just as tasty as the rest). Add the lot to a food processor and whizz until reduced to a rice-like grain. Heat 2 tablespoons of olive oil in a frying pan and add the cauliflower when the oil is piping hot. Then add the garlic, the rosemary and a little pepper and salt. Stir-fry for a few minutes and then set aside to cool, preferably in the fridge and with a lid on the pan. In the meantime, wash the endive and pat dry with a tea towel. Chop the endive into thin slices and mix together all the ingredients for the dressing. When the cauliflower rice has cooled (it doesn't have to be completely chilled, just cold enough so that the endive doesn't wilt) stir it and the beans into the raw endive. Add the dressing just before serving.

In the afternoon

Sublime parsley and red onion
SALAD

Flat leaf parsley is so much more than just a fancy garnish. I adore parsley, and it has a lot more qualities than you might think. Long ago, parsley was known primarily for its medicinal properties and not as a cooking ingredient. It contains more iron than spinach so is excellent for combatting anaemia. It also stimulates the body's own production of vitamin B_{12}, which is particularly important for vegetarians. This salad is delicious with risotto, too. Don't forget to use a very good-quality olive oil.

serves *2* | preparation time *10* minutes

2 large handfuls of flat leaf parsley
¼ red onion, in half rings
3 tbsp extra virgin olive oil
2 tsp lemon juice
¼ tsp sea salt and freshly ground black pepper

Stir all the ingredients together and season with salt and pepper.

In the afternoon

RAW BEETROOT

with buffalo mozzarella

Personally speaking, I much prefer raw beetroot to the mush you get when you cook it, though I will admit to a weakness for my mother's mashed version. Raw beetroot is the real deal, though. It's got bite and a refreshing kind of sweetness, and you can combine it with almost anything. A salad containing several different coloured beetroots looks and taste just heavenly. This dish is great as a starter or a side dish.

serves *4* | preparation time *15* minutes

2 raw beetroots (different colours), not too large
2 balls of fresh buffalo mozzarella (or burrata)
1 grapefruit, skinned and in segments
1 tsp chilli flakes
2 tsp fresh dill, finely chopped

½ handful fresh mint, finely chopped
2 tbsp extra virgin olive oil
2 tbsp hazelnut oil
½ tsp Himalayan or sea salt and freshly ground
   black pepper

Peel, then thinly slice the beetroot. Tear up the mozzarella and place in a bowl. Peel the grapefruit, cut out the segments and add to the mozzarella. Then add the beetroot, chilli flakes and the fresh herbs and. Sprinkle with the olive and hazelnut oils and season with salt and pepper.

In the afternoon

GREEN PANCAKES

Green pancakes first appeared in our house when my older children started to come home from school for their lunch and they were always delighted when I served this particular treat. The pancakes are not only delicious, but they're very easy to make, too. All you need to do is make a pancake mix using fresh and (better still, organic) ingredients – including a high-quality wholemeal flour – and then throw in a few large handfuls of fresh spinach. At a stroke, you rehabilitate the poor pancake from its undeserved status as an unhealthy food. I like to use unsweetened organic soya milk, but you can use other kinds of milk too, even just plain old 'ordinary' milk.

serves *12* | preparation time *30* minutes

300 g wholemeal flour
700 ml organic (soya) milk
1 tsp salt
2 eggs
3 large handfuls of spinach
olive oil for frying
1 block of young cheese

Whisk the flour with the milk, salt and eggs. Add the spinach and mix using a hand blender until smooth and green. Heat a little olive oil in a frying pan and fry each pancake until golden brown on both sides. When the pancake is almost done, place the slices of cheese on one half and fold over. Reduce the heat, cover and allow the cheese to melt. Repeat for the rest of the pancake mix.

In the afternoon

Stuffed
SWEET POTATO
with remoulade sauce

I once almost fell into a deep depression after a health expert told me that I should stop eating avocados because they were disrupting my body's hormonal balance. The avocado is by far my favourite fruit – or vegetable, depending on your perspective and how you eat it. I was used to eating at least one a day and now I had to sit there munching on a carrot watching the rest of my family indulge themselves in my favourite food. 'Hate' may be too strong a word for what I felt, but it wasn't far from the truth. However, when I finally realised that not eating avocados was doing me more harm than good, I started eating them again – and without any ill effects either, touch wood.

serves *2* | preparation time *50* minutes (incl. oven time)

Stuffed sweet potato
1 large or 2 small sweet potatoes, skins on, washed
½ chilli pepper, deseeded and chopped into thin
   rings
¼ red onion, diced
2 tbsp red cabbage, very finely chopped
½ avocado, chopped
1 tomato, deseeded and chopped into small pieces
4 heaped tbsp black beans (from a jar/tin), drained
1 handful coriander
1 tsp chilli flakes
1 lime, halved

Remoulade sauce
juice of 1 lemon
½ tsp salt
1 tsp coarse-grain mustard
50 ml extra virgin olive oil
2 heaped tbsp yoghurt
1 tbsp flat leaf parsley, finely chopped
1 tbsp finely chopped chives
2 tbsp capers
4 tbsp mayonnaise
2 tbsp finely chopped gherkins
freshly ground black pepper

Preheat the oven to 200 °C. Place the sweet potatoes whole in an oven dish and put them in the oven. Bake for 45 minutes until soft. Wash and prepare all of the vegetables for the filling (chilli pepper, onion, red cabbage, avocado, tomato). Then make the remoulade sauce by mixing all of the ingredients together. After 45 minutes, take the potatoes out of the oven, set aside for a while to cool (they will be piping hot) and then cut them open and fill them with the beans and finely chopped vegetables. Pour the remoulade sauce over the stuffed sweet potatoes, sprinkle with coriander and chilli flakes, and squeeze over a few drops of lime juice. The potatoes are fantastic served with a fresh green salad.

In the afternoon

VEG

with Nan's dip

I could go on and on about this or that dish being the best thing I have ever tasted, but you will just have to believe me. Regardless of your tastes, the dip sauce below is so good that it would turn even the most hardened veggie-hater into a carrot-lover. That includes my kids, with their insatiable appetite for 'unhealthy stuff', whom I try to feed with as much nutrients as possible without having to resort to brute force. Fortunately, I have a secret weapon: my friend Nan, who has been making this snack since long before we met. Nowadays, her 'Veg with Nan's dip' is ever-present in our house whenever we throw a party or even just when the kids get home from school. I must admit, however, that it took me a lot of practice before I finally managed to make Nan's simple but fantastic sauce as delicious as she does herself. For many years, I was used to hearing: 'Mmm, not bad Mum, but not as good as Nan's, is it?' Immensely frustrating, I don't mind saying. But in the end, after much trial and error, I succeeded!

serves *6* | preparation time *20* minutes

Vegetables
½ cucumber, chopped into blocks of about
   7 cm and then into strips
a few stalks of celery, chopped into pieces
   about 7 cm long
½ broccoli, cut into florets
¼ cauliflower, cut into florets
a bowl of radishes
8 (baby) carrots (or chop up larger carrots
   like you did the cucumber)

Nan's dip
4 full tbsp organic mayonnaise
2 full tbsp crème fraîche
2 tbsp finely chopped chives
½ tsp salt
½ tsp freshly ground black pepper
1 clove of garlic, minced

Wash the vegetables, chop as required and mix all the ingredients for the dip sauce together. Serve on a chopping board or a nice plate and dig in!

In the afternoon

Spanish
MEGA-BEAN SALAD
with avocado and sesame oil

My brother, Niels, often comes to visit us for a week or two and we usually end up chatting non-stop about food because we love cooking together and creating new recipes (I kid you not!). The last time he was here he conjured up this fantastic salad with Spanish white beans, which you can buy outside of Spain too, thankfully. These beans are extremely versatile and can be used in all kinds of salads.

serves *4* | preparation time *35* minutes

Salad
300 g Spanish white beans
half punnet of cherry tomatoes
1 red pepper
1 yellow pepper
2 red onions
1 cucumber, deseeded
1 avocado
10 sprigs of chives
1 handful of coriander
½ lemon, just the juice

Dressing
pinch of salt and pepper
2 tsp walnut oil
1 tbsp white balsamic vinegar
1½ tbsp sesame oil
2 tbsp olive oil

Mix together all the ingredients for the dressing and set aside. Rinse the beans well and leave to dry. Chop the peppers, cucumber and avocado into equal-sized pieces. Halve the cherry tomatoes and slice the onion into thin rings. Mix everything together in a large bowl. Chop the coriander and the chives and stir into the salad. Sprinkle with the dressing and a little lemon juice.

In the afternoon

Packed
SAVOURY TART

The variations on this kind of tart are endless as you can literally add anything you like, so it's guaranteed to meet with approval. It's easy to make and great as a quick snack or for a picnic. Just make sure you pre-bake the pastry, otherwise it can get a bit soggy. The trick is to keep the ingredients for the filling nice and light.

serves *4-6* | preparation time *35* minutes

1 large roll of puff pastry
1 small aubergine
½ courgette
250 g mini pomodori tomatoes
4 tbsp olive oil
2 tsp dried oregano
2 tsp dried thyme

250 g ricotta
zest of 1 lemon
1 handful fresh basil
sea salt and freshly ground black pepper
a few sprigs of fresh thyme for garnishing
Extra equipment: steam basket, baking paper

Preheat the oven to 150°C. Roll out the pastry out and place it on baking paper on an oven tray). Score a line along the pastry 1 cm from the edge, don't cut through to the bottom; this will give a nice rectangle shape to the pastry and a crisp, clean edge. Prick a few holes in the centre of the rectangle using a fork to help keep the pasty nice and light. Bake the pastry in the oven for about 8 minutes, then remove it from the oven. In the meantime prepare the vegetable filling. You will need to steam the aubergine, otherwise it will become too dry. Cut it in half lengthways and then slice the halves into long strips – 4 per half. Bring a saucepan of water to the boil with 2 teaspoons of salt and steam the aubergine for about 7 minutes in a steam basket if you have one or use a colander and the lid of the saucepan. Chop the courgette into 1 cm cubes and halve the tomatoes. Add the olive oil, 1 teaspoon of oregano and 1 teaspoon of thyme, then half a teaspoon of salt and plenty of pepper. Give it all a good stir. When the aubergine is cooked, chop it up into small pieces and add to the tomato-courgette mix. Then mix the ricotta with the lemon zest, 1 teaspoon of oregano, 1 teaspoon of thyme, ½ teaspoon of salt and black pepper. Spread the vegetable mix over the rectangular section of the tart and top off with the ricotta mix. Return it to the oven and bake for 20 minutes. Chop the basil into thin strips. Garnish the tart with the basil and the sprigs of thyme and serve.

In the afternoon

Roasted
CAESAR SALAD

Now don't get me wrong. I'm not saying that your 'normal' Caesar salad is boring or anything like that. I love a good, crispy Caesar salad – it's the one salad that is always sure to please (except for the McDonald's version...) and I have eaten my fair share of them at one of my favourite restaurants in Amsterdam, a place called 'George' where they are amazing. But this version of the Caesar salad is at the very least 'interesting'. It is just as good as the original of the species, but 100 percent vegetarian, of course. Which brings me to the next question: why the need for anchovies in the first place? In this recipe the salty flavour comes from the Parmesan cheese and a sprinkling of nutritional yeast flakes* (I had to include these in the book one way or another).

serves *2* | preparation time *20* minutes

Caesar salad
2 eggs
4 tbsp olive oil
1 clove of garlic, crushed
2 'little gem' lettuces or small heads of romaine lettuce, halved
2 slices crusty wholemeal bread, torn into large croutons
1 block Parmesan cheese
sea salt and freshly ground black pepper

Dressing
2 tbsp organic mayonnaise
2 tsp Dijon mustard
½ lime, just the juice
3 tbsp extra virgin olive oil
½ clove of garlic, crushed
2 tsp finely grated Parmesan cheese
2 tsp nutritional yeast flakes
sea salt and freshly ground black pepper

Place the eggs in a saucepan with cold water and a pinch of salt and bring to the boil. Boil for 9 minutes and then run under ice-cold water. In the meantime, make the dressing by putting all the ingredients in a jar and giving it a good shake. Then mix the olive oil with the garlic and spread some over the halved heads of lettuce. Preheat the oven to 200°C. Spread the remaining oil and garlic mixture over the bread croutons, season with salt then bake until nice and crispy. Heat a griddle pan and cook the lettuce halves gems on both sides on a high heat for a few minutes until they start to brown (but not for too long, or they will go all limp on you). Place 2 half heads of lettuce on each plate and grate plenty of Parmesan cheese on top. Peel the eggs, halve them and put one egg on each plate. Season with salt and pepper, top off with the croutons and sprinkle with the Caesar dressing.

———————— Nutritional yeast is a deactivated yeast. It is rich in vitamin B_{12} and is also a whole protein because it contains all eight essential amino acids. It doesn't contain any sugar or gluten and almost no fat or sodium. Vegans use it primarily as a substitute for cheese because of its salty, Parmesan-like taste. The most important thing, however, is that it is quite delicious.

In the afternoon

HEIRLOOM TOMATOES

Heirloom is a word used to describe fruit and vegetables with a long history but that are nowadays only grown sporadically. Like the large heirloom tomatoes in this recipe, they can be difficult, but not impossible, to find. Keep an eye out for them because they sometimes appear out of nowhere at your local market or even in the supermarket. If you happen to spot them, don't go home without them. I used to make this salad a lot when we lived in Amsterdam, especially when the first rays of the summer sun hit our faces and we would frantically dig out the picnic basket and wine cooler and make our way to the nearest park. With their funny shape, heirloom tomatoes look a bit like wild flowers when you cut them open, and that is exactly what makes this salad so lovely and summery.

serves *4-6* | preparation time *25* minutes

Tomato salad
1 medium-sized red onion, halved and sliced
   into thin rings
dash of red wine vinegar
1 cucumber, deseeded and chopped into small
   pieces
2 large heirloom tomatoes, in nice thin slices
6 pomodori (or other ripe tomatoes), sliced
250 g mini pomodori or cherry tomatoes, halved
15 g chives, chopped into 1½ cm pieces
15 g fresh dill, chopped into 1½ cm pieces,
   or 2 tbsp dried dill
15 g fresh coriander, leaves plucked and stems
   finely chopped
15 g flat leaf parsley, leaves only

15 g fresh tarragon, finely chopped, or 2 tbsp dried
   tarragon
1 clove of garlic, very finely chopped or crushed

Dressing
40 ml lemon juice
40 ml red wine vinegar
60 ml extra virgin olive oil
1 tsp mustard
2 tsp honey
1 tsp sea salt and freshly ground black pepper

Put the onion rings, along with a dash of vinegar, in a bowl and leave to soak for 20 minutes. Then drain well with a colander. Using your hands, toss the onion, cucumber and tomatoes (all three kinds) together and arrange on a large shallow tray or dish. Mix the ingredients for the dressing together, then add it to the salad. Finally, add the herbs and garlic and toss once more.

In the afternoon

Fantastic
EGG SALAD

We usually make this egg salad during the summer when we have guests staying over, and believe me that happens a lot! At eight o'clock in the morning, the ladies are often to be found holding court in the kitchen and making an enormous breakfast for the whole gang. This salad is a permanent feature on those mornings, not forgetting, of course, the fresh bread dutifully collected by 'the men of the house'. All very clichéed, but sometimes that is exactly what one needs in life.

serves *6-8* | preparation time *15* minutes

1 tsp salt
8 medium-sized eggs
2 handfuls fresh flat leaf parsley, finely chopped
½ red onion
20 small gherkins, or 1 large handful

3 tbsp mayonnaise
2 large tsp Dijon mustard
sea salt and freshly ground pepper

Hard-boil the eggs by putting them in a saucepan of cold water with 1 teaspoon of salt and cooking them for exactly 12 minutes from the moment they begin to boil (set a timer). While they are boiling, chop the parsley; use some of the thinner stalks as well if you like, but throw away the thick ones. Dice the onion and chop the gherkins into thin slices. Mix everything together in a large bowl and add the mayonnaise and the mustard. Peel the eggs and slice use an egg slicer or a very sharp knife. Add to the mayo-mix and season with salt and pepper.

In the afternoon

Roasted
CARROT SALAD
with sourdough bread, young peas and parsley pesto

A few years back we celebrated Christmas together with Nicholas's family. It was a huge gathering with an abundance of delicious food. It was also the first time I had quinoa, in this instance in a fabulous salad with carrot, mint, feta and walnuts, and I became a fan immediately. Later, just so that I wouldn't find myself gobbling down the same quinoa dish every single day (I had no objection to this myself, but the rest of my family begged to differ), I came up with this variation. This light and fresh dish is perfect for (spring) brunches.

serves *2-4* | preparation time *35* minutes

Carrot salad
100 g sourdough bread
10 baby carrots (or 'ordinary' carrots chopped into
  strips), cleaned
4 tbsp olive oil for cooking
sea salt and freshly ground black pepper
1 clove of garlic, crushed
200 g fresh peas (in their pods or not, you choose)
100 g mixed salad
1 handful fresh mint
80 g walnuts, crushed
50 g feta

Parsley-pesto dressing
40 g fresh flat leaf parsley, finely chopped
40 g grated Parmesan cheese
1 clove of garlic, crushed
120 ml extra virgin olive oil, plus extra for serving
1 lemon, the zest and half of the juice
½ tsp sea salt and freshly ground black pepper

Preheat the oven to 200°C. Tear the bread into pieces and toss with the carrots, the olive oil, a little salt and pepper and the crushed garlic. Place in an oven dish or on a baking tray covered with baking paper and bake for 10–15 minutes until you have crunchy croutons and lightly browned carrots. Give everything a good toss every now and then. If you have been able to find peas still in their pods, cook these for about 1 minute (you don't need to cook peas not in their pods). Have a bowl of ice-cold water at the ready into which you can drain the peas when cooked so that they will retain their nice green colour. Drain again in a colander after a few minutes. Get a nice flat tray or dish on which to serve your salad. Open the pods with a knife, but do not remove the peas. Arrange all of the ingredients on the serving dish – the salad leaves, carrots, croutons, mint, walnuts, feta and peas (with or without pods). Season with salt and pepper. Sprinkle with the dressing and serve along with some extra dressing and extra virgin olive oil.

In the afternoon

Salad
"LA PALOMA"

La Paloma is a fabulous restaurant here in Ibiza that serves Israeli food during the day and Italian in the evenings. I love going there for lunch and enjoying the beautiful garden, the smell of the orange trees and the amazing aromas coming from the kitchen. One of my favourite salads at La Paloma is their soba noodle salad with fresh, crispy vegetables and a tahini dressing. My version is not exactly a carbon copy, but I think it's close. It does take a bit of time to prepare, but it's more than worth the effort.

serves *2-4* | preparation time *35* minutes

For the salad
200 g soba noodles
2 tbsp olive oil
2 parsnips, sliced lengthways into strips
8 stalks green asparagus, hard ends trimmed off
sea salt and freshly ground black pepper
150 g French beans, ends trimmed
150 g broccoli, cut into florets
150 g roman cauliflower (or ordinary cauliflower)
  cut into florets
150 g carrots, sliced
150 g red cabbage
1 avocado, peeled and sliced

1 mango, in pieces
2 handfuls fresh spinach
chilli flakes

For the dressing
60 ml tahini paste
3 tbsp extra virgin olive oil
60 ml water
1½ lemon, squeezed
2 tsp sea salt
2 cloves of garlic, crushed
3 tsp honey
freshly ground black pepper

Preheat the oven to 200°C. Cook the soba noodles according to the instructions and rinse thoroughly with cold water so that they don't stick together. Stir in a tablespoon of olive oil and set aside. Mix the parsnip and the asparagus with a tablespoon of olive oil and a little salt and pepper. Place them on a baking tray and cook them in the oven for 10–15 minutes, stirring around occasionally. Bring a saucepan of water with a pinch of salt to the boil. Using a steam basket or a colander and the lid of the saucepan, steam the beans, broccoli and cauliflower for about 7 minutes until done. Dunk the beans in a bowl of ice-cold water briefly so that they retain their green colour. Heat 1 tablespoon of olive oil and fry the carrot for about 2 minutes; remove and set aside. Season with salt and pepper. Slice the red cabbage into strips and fry for 2–3 minutes in the same pan. Make the dressing by mixing all the ingredients together in a jar, put the lid on and give it a good shake. Place the noodles in the middle of the plates and surround with the fried, steamed and roasted vegetables. Add the avocado, mango and spinach. Sprinkle with chilli flakes and serve with an individual helping of dressing.

In the afternoon

Salad of raw
BRUSSELS SPROUTS
and broad beans

I came across this fantastic recipe entirely by accident when I was looking for a good way to roast Brussels sprouts. Sprouts are delicious roasted in the oven, but they're even better raw. I've always loved sprouts, especially when my mother mashed them together with potatoes, although this was partly because mash was the only thing she was ever any good at making (apart from her spaghetti Bolognese maybe), sorry mum, but I have to be honest. As a result, I could never understand why other kids had such an aversion to sprouts. I tried stir-frying, griddling and steaming sprouts. All mildly unsatisfactory until one day I chopped them up very small and was about to slide them into oven, only to be stopped in my tracks after having a quick taste to see if they needed anything extra. The raw sprouts were so delicious that they didn't even make it into the oven.

serves *4* | preparation time *20* minutes

200 g broad beans
250 g Brussels sprouts
3 small dried chilli peppers, finely chopped,
   or 1½ tsp chilli flakes
large handful fresh flat leaf parsley, finely chopped
small handful fresh coriander, leaves only

60 ml extra virgin olive oil
1 lemon, the zest and half of the juice
40 g grated Parmesan cheese
sea salt and freshly ground black pepper

Bring a saucepan of water to the boil, add the broad beans and blanch for 1 or 2 minutes. Drain and set aside to cool. Using a sharp knife, cut an opening in the outer skin and pop out the bean; repeat until you have skinned all the beans. Trim off the outer leaves from the sprouts and chop finely. Mix the sprouts, broad beans, chilli peppers, coriander, parsley, olive oil, lemon juice and lemon zest together. Put everything into a salad bowl, season with salt and pepper and sprinkle with the Parmesan cheese.

In the afternoon

Large mixed
SPRING SALAD

A large mixed salad is probably the best thing you can make on a hot, sunny day, and the more colours the better, because that means more vitamins. Mixed salads basically allow you to do whatever you like and you never need to stick to the recipe. Just look to see what is available, either in your own garden or in the shops – and remember, the fresher the better.

serves *2* | preparation time *20* minutes

Salad
2 eggs
8 stalks green asparagus
2 tsp olive oil for griddling
3 heads of lettuce (little gem)
4 radishes
1 avocado
¼ red onion, in thin rings
1 handful beetroot shoots
10 Kalamata olives, deseeded and halved
½ handful walnuts, crushed
1 (yellow) tomato, sliced
handful of yellow cherry tomatoes, halved

Dressing
60 ml extra virgin olive oil
juice of ½ lemon
1 large tsp mayonnaise
1 large tsp Dijon mustard
1 tsp honey
½ tsp Himalayan or sea salt
lots of freshly ground black pepper
1 clove of garlic, crushed

Put all the ingredients for the vinaigrette in a jar and shake vigorously. Place the eggs in a saucepan of cold water with 1 teaspoon of salt and bring to the boil. Leave to boil for 9 minutes and then run under ice-cold water. Trim off the hard ends of the asparagus, coat them with olive oil and cook on a griddle pan for 5–7 minutes, turning occasionally. Pull the lettuces apart, wash the leaves, and pat dry. Thinly slice the radishes. Peel and halve the avocado and chop into slices. Arrange all the ingredients neatly on two plates. Start with the salad leaves, then add the avocado, radishes, onion, beetroot shoots, olives, walnuts, tomatoes and finally the asparagus and the quartered eggs. Sprinkle the dressing over the salad.

In the afternoon

Japanese
GLASS NOODLE
salad

A few years ago I interviewed the very successful Australian culinary author Annabel Langbein when she came to give a cooking workshop in a bookshop in Amsterdam. With consummate ease she made one delicious dish after another while we all 'oohed' and 'aahed' in unison. It was all just fabulous and fresh and oh so very simple – at least if you knew what you were doing. And it was no different when it came to the spring rolls she made that afternoon either. I had never tasted anything like them, my only point of reference being the deep-fried version popular at Vietnamese food stalls in the Netherlands. Annabel Langbein's were lighter, fresher, crispier. Even though she used prawns in her spring rolls and I'm not big on prawns, the recipe stuck in my mind and I decided to make my own, slightly different, vegetarian variation. A little simpler, but delicious nonetheless. You can use all of the ingredients that I use in this salad to make spring rolls like Annabel's, too, if you wish.

serves *3-4* | preparation time *20* minutes

Salad
100 g glass noodles, cooked and drained
8 stalks green asparagus
2 eggs
1 tbsp soya sauce
1 tbsp olive oil for frying
1 avocado, cut in half and sliced lengthways
½ cucumber, deseeded and chopped into thick 'matchsticks'
1 handful coriander, leaves only
1 small handful mint, leaves only
1 small handful basil, leaves only, chopped

Soya dressing (or dip for spring rolls)
6 tbsp soya sauce
1 tbsp sesame oil
¼ red onion, diced
3 tbsp rice vinegar
2 tsp honey
4 tbsp sweet chilli sauce
freshly ground black pepper

Cook the noodles according to the instructions. Drain and set aside to cool. Mix all the ingredients for the soya dressing and set aside. Trim the hard ends off the asparagus and chop into 2 cm pieces. Steam for 5 minutes over boiling water with a pinch of salt (use a steam basket or a colander with a saucepan lid). Whisk the eggs together with the soya sauce and fry in the olive oil until you have an omelette. Fold over twice, as quickly as possible, and continue frying until done. Slice into strips about 3 mm thick. Toss all the vegetables carefully with the noodles and then top off with the omelette strips. Garnish with the herbs and sprinkle with the dressing just before serving.

In the afternoon

WATERMELON SALAD

with mango, feta and mint

This salad is so refreshing and tasty that you will probably want to make it all summer long! Watermelons are fantastic thirst quenchers and almost everyone likes them. When combined with the aromatic taste of mango, salty feta and fresh mint, the result is a serious explosion of taste, not to mention the fabulous display of colour on your plate.

for *1* large bowl | preparation time *10* minutes

½ watermelon
2 mangoes
150 g feta
2 limes, zest and juice
½ red onion, in thin rings
1 chilli pepper, deseeded and finely chopped

60 ml extra virgin olive oil
½ tsp sea salt and freshly ground black pepper
1 handful fresh mint, leaves only, finely chopped

Slice the watermelon into nice small pieces, do the same with the mangoes and the feta and then add the lot to a large bowl. Grate the zest of the limes and then squeeze out the juice. Add the onion, chilli pepper, lime zest and juice to the bowl and season with salt and pepper. Chop the mint into thin strips and add to the bowl along with the olive oil. Mix well together and add a little extra salt and pepper if required – the taste should literally explode in your mouth.

In the afternoon

Green salad with
EDAMAME BEANS
and warm caper vinaigrette

What can I say about green salads that hasn't been said many times before? Maybe that they are always either fantastic or excruciatingly boring. The latter is a real and needless pity, and you can still go into a restaurant these days and be served a lifeless and loveless green salad. It's often just a pile of green leaves and an instruction to use as much oil and vinegar as you like – thanks, but I'll pass. I know that a simple green salad can be delicious, but sometimes all it takes is a little more love and attention. This is a very simple recipe, but one with a high impact.

serves *2* | preparation time *15* minutes

Green salad
150 g French beans, ends trimmed
100 g edamame beans
2 eggs
3 heads of lettuce (little gem)
2 large tbsp Parmesan cheese
sea salt
toast (optional)

Warm caper dressing
2 tbsp capers
1 lemon
60 ml olive oil
1 tsp honey
½ tsp sea salt
freshly ground black pepper

Cook the French beans in boiling water with a little salt for 5 minutes until done. After draining, run them under ice-cold water so that they retain their nice green colour. Cook the edamame beans for 4 minutes with a pinch of salt, making sure that they still have a little bite; you don't want them to be limp. Put the eggs in a saucepan of cold water, add a pinch of salt and bring to the boil. Boil them for 9 minutes (or 11–12 minutes if you want your eggs to be rock hard), then run them under cold water; halve them when they are cool enough. Chop the ends off the heads of lettuce, pull off the leaves, wash them and pat dry. Divide over two plates. Add the edamame beans, French beans and halved eggs. Make the dressing. Peel the lemon and scoop the flesh into a small saucepan, add the capers and a little salt and pepper and place on a medium heat. Stir for 5 minutes, remove from the heat and add a teaspoon of honey and the olive oil. Add more salt and pepper if you wish and mix well. Drizzle the dressing over the salad and top off with the Parmesan cheese. Try serving the salad with a slice of toast.

Farmer's
QUINOA TART

Not so long ago, 'recipe bloggerland' was swamped by a brand-new craze: kale – it was all 'kale' this and 'kale' that. Why all the fuss about something as commonplace as cabbage? Hadn't we been eating it for years already, with nothing fancier than spuds and gravy? Well, it turned out we were all wrong. Kale was a very special vegetable, and one that lends itself to endless experimentation and variation. My first kale chips burned to a cinder during experiment number one, but I didn't give up and by the fifth attempt they were even edible. I threw everything I could into the mix – chilli peppers, Parmesan cheese, olive oil and herbs – you name it I tried it. At one stage I even had my whole family eating raw 'massaged' kale salad. But I'm being side-tracked. I did find that kale and quinoa proved a fabulous combination. So, I had to devise a recipe that I hadn't seen anywhere else before. The result below has become a permanent feature of my cooking arsenal.

serves *4-6* | preparation time *50* minutes

200 g quinoa
4 tbsp olive oil
2 medium-sized red onions, diced
2 cloves of garlic, finely chopped
200 g finely chopped kale
6 eggs
225 ml (soya) cream, for cooking
100 g grated cheddar cheese

100 g Parmesan cheese
1 tbsp butter or oil for greasing the oven dish
125 g soft goat's cheese
1 tsp chilli flakes
1 tsp sea salt and freshly ground black pepper

Preheat the oven to 180 °C. Wash and cook the quinoa in water (2 parts water to 1 part quinoa) with 1 teaspoon of salt. In the meantime, fry the onion in the olive oil, stirring continuously for about 5 minutes, until soft. Add the garlic for the last minute of frying. Add the kale and fry for another 5 minutes. While the kale is frying, beat the eggs with the cream and then add the cheddar and Parmesan cheese, plus the chilli flakes and a twist of salt and pepper. Combine this with the kale and the quinoa and spoon everything into a greased oven dish. Crumble the goat's cheese on top, cover the entire dish with aluminium foil and place in the oven for 30 minutes. The result will be a delicious kale and quinoa tart, or flan.

In the afternoon

WATER

Water is probably the most important ingredient in this book. Sounds odd I know, but think about it for a minute: we cannot survive without water. Our bodies consist mostly of water (men approx. 63 percent and women approx. 52 percent) and we have to keep that level topped up every day. We need to consume around 2½ litres of fluids a day, most of which we then dispose of again through sweating. Not all the water that we take on board comes through drinking – about 1 litre comes from the food we eat. However, we still need to drink at least 1½ litres a day just to keep our bodies healthy and to prevent dehydration.

You can't beat pure water, but you can also pimp it a little by adding some natural and simple ingredients, which can help to ensure that you drink enough each day. Leave the water to stand for at least two hours in the fridge before you drink it to allow the flavours to develop.

Spanish love
Water with orange and lemon slices: 1 litre water, 1 orange, 1 lemon

Steve Jobs with basil
Water with apple and basil: 1 litre water, 1 apple in slices, 2 large handfuls of basil

Cucumber - straight up
Water with cucumber: 1 litre water, ½ cucumber in long slices

Ginger mint
Water with ginger'n'mint: 1 litre water, 5 cm ginger peeled and sliced, 3 sprigs of mint

In mint condition
Water with mint and lime: 1 litre water, 3 sprigs of mint, 1 lime in slices

Beautiful rosemary
Water with rosemary and raspberries: 1 litre water, 5 sprigs of rosemary, ½ punnet of raspberries

SOUP

whenever you feel like it

The fact that I have dedicated a whole chapter to soup is not just because I am a huge fan, but also because I don't think you can split soup up into 'lunch' and 'dinner' – I've even been known to sit down to a hot bowl of soup in the morning. I do it every now and then at the weekend when the rest of the family is still asleep and I have those magical first few hours of the day all to myself. There is just something snug and warm about soup, although I admit that since we moved to Ibiza I have also experimented a lot with cold gazpachos. When it hits 40°C here, a cold soup can be very invigorating and provide you with a much-needed energy boost. Of course, you also have your typical winter soups that fill the house with their warm aroma when it is freezing cold and wet or stormy outside. Or you can enjoy soups made from spring or summer vegetables while sitting in the garden in the late evening sun. So, whether as a starter, a side dish or a main meal, in the morning, afternoon or evening and in spring, summer, autumn or winter... there is always time for soup.

POTAGE

de vigilia

This is a fantastic soup that we first tasted as a 'soppas del dia' (soup of the day) at the local tavern in the village at the foot of the mountain, where they literally have a different soup for each day of the week. I know, for example, that they always serve chick pea soup on Thursdays, that Wednesday is fish soup day and Mondays are reserved for lentil soup – they even serve a vegetarian paella on Fridays. We often drop in for a bowl of soup when we are picking the kids up from school. With the help of a lot of sign language I have slowly but surely been able to discover what they put in their potage de vigilia – one of the most important ingredients is the olive oil that is added at the very last minute. After much trial and error, I think that this recipe does it justice, more or less...

serves *6* | preparation time *60* minutes

4 eggs
1½ litres vegetable stock (4 cubes)
2 medium-sized white onions, diced
3 tbsp olive oil for frying
1½ tsp curry powder
1 tsp paprika powder
½ tsp ginger powder
1 tsp turmeric powder
2 tsp cumin powder
3 large cloves of garlic, thinly sliced
1 courgette, chopped into small pieces

2 large potatoes, peeled and chopped into small pieces
800 g chickpeas (from a jar/tin), drained
200 g green or French beans, trimmed and chopped into 2 cm pieces
200 g spinach, finely chopped
80 ml extra virgin olive oil
3 tsp sea salt
lots of freshly ground black pepper
wholemeal bread (optional)

Put the eggs in a saucepan of cold water, add a pinch of salt, boil for 11 minutes and run under ice-cold water when done. Make the stock and leave it simmering on a low heat. In the meantime, fry the onion in 3 tablespoons of olive oil in a large frying pan on a high heat. Turn down the heat after a few minutes and add the spices (curry powder, paprika, ginger, turmeric, and cumin) and the garlic. Fry for a few more minutes until the onion is nice and soft, but make sure that you don't burn the spices. Add the courgette, potatoes, chickpeas and beans and continue frying for another 5 minutes. Then add the stock to the vegetables and bring to the boil. Leave to simmer for 30 minutes with a lid on the pan. Finally, add the spinach, bring to the boil again, cover and leave to simmer for another 10 minutes. Remove from the heat and add the extra virgin olive oil and a little salt and pepper. Finely chop the eggs and add them to the soup. Season to taste with salt and pepper and serve with wholemeal bread (optional).

Soup whenever you feel like it

French
ONION SOUP
from the garden

I can remember eating French onion soup quite often when I was younger and that I loved it. However, at some point or other it suddenly vanished from menus everywhere never to reappear. Too old-fashioned, I suppose. But last summer, when I saw that I had a major surplus of lovely looking onions in the garden, so I figured it was the perfect moment for a French onion soup revival and I set about making it myself – but this time under the Spanish sun.

serves *4* | preparation time *40* minutes

1 litre vegetable stock (2 cubes)
6 medium-sized onions
2 tbsp butter
3 bay leaves
4 tbsp thyme (dried or fresh)
500 ml dry white wine (for example, Verdejo)

sea salt and freshly ground black pepper
Parmesan cheese for garnishing

Make the vegetable stock. Chop the onions in half and slice into thin rings. Melt the butter in a heavy-based saucepan, then add the onions. Reduce the heat and stir the onions well with the butter. Place a lid on the saucepan and leave the onions to caramelise for about 20 minutes until they are light brown in colour; stir every now and then and add some more butter if you think the onions are becoming too dry. Half way through cooking the onions, heat up the stock and add the bay leaf and thyme. When the onions are done add the stock to the pan. Bring to the boil and add the white wine. Cook the soup for a further 10 minutes, uncovered, and then season with salt and pepper. Pour the soup into your best soup bowls, garnish with Parmesan cheese shavings and serve immediately.

Soup whenever you feel like it

Green
GAZPACHO

This gazpacho is refreshing and delicious and we make it frequently in the summer. The great thing about gazpacho is that all of the ingredients are used raw and so they retain all of their vitamins – and once your children get to like it, you won't be able to make it often enough. I wanted to try something different from the traditional gazpacho, which is made from tomatoes and therefore red in colour. The addition of avocado here makes the soup irresistibly creamy, and they are an excellent source of nutrients for vegetarians. Apart from being full of good fats, vitamins and fibre, avocados also contain all eight essential amino acids needed to form complete proteins.

serves *6* | preparation time *35* minutes (plus 1 hour in the fridge)

Gazpacho
1 litre vegetable stock (3 cubes), cooled
2 green peppers, cleaned and chopped
1½ cucumber, unpeeled, in slices
1 avocado, peeled and deseeded, chopped
½ courgette, sliced
1 medium-sized white onion, halved and sliced
  into rings
1 large clove of garlic, crushed
1 large handful fresh coriander, finely chopped
120 ml extra virgin olive oil

60 ml apple cider vinegar
1 tsp sea salt and freshly ground black pepper

Fresh salsa
3 tomatoes
½ cucumber
½ red onion
1 handful fresh coriander, finely chopped
2 tbsp extra virgin olive oil
½ tsp sea salt and freshly ground black pepper

Make the stock and leave to cool for 30 minutes. In the meantime, wash and prepare all the vegetables so that they fit easily into a blender. Then make the salsa. Score the skins of the tomatoes and place them in boiling water for one minute so that they are easier to peel. Remove the skin and the seeds and chop them into very small pieces. Peel and deseed the cucumber and chop up very small. Dice the red onion and put into a bowl with the tomatoes and cucumber. Add the coriander and olive oil, mix well and season the salsa with salt and pepper. Pour half of the stock into a blender and then add the ingredients for the soup (retain a little of the olive oil). Mix together until thick and smooth and return the mix to the saucepan with the rest of the stock. Give it all a good stir, cover and place in the fridge for at least one hour, together with the salsa. Pour the cold soup into bowls then add 2 or 3 tablespoons of salsa to each one. Sprinkle a little extra virgin olive oil on top and serve.

Soup whenever you feel like it

MUSTARD SOUP

with orange and sweet potato

When I was 16 years old, my brother asked me to help with a big Christmas dinner he had organised. For one evening only he had transformed an old hospital in Amsterdam into a spectacular restaurant complete with linen tablecloths and 80 handpicked guests. I was one of the waitresses and I still remember how excited I was just to be present at such a special occasion. We served a three-course dinner and rushed around all evening. Whenever we had a minute to spare we grabbed a quick bite to eat in the kitchen to keep us going. One of the things I remember best about that evening is the fabulous aroma of the mustard and orange soup that bubbled away all night on the stove. So, for me, this soup is a real trip down memory lane.

serves *4* | preparation time *20* minutes

1 litre vegetable stock (3 cubes)
1 medium-sized onion
3 tbsp olive oil for frying
1 large sweet potato, cut into small pieces
1 tsp turmeric
3 tbsp coarse-grain mustard

125 ml (soya) cream
juice of 1 orange
1/2 tsp sea salt
Freshly ground black pepper
1 handful flat leaf parsley, chopped

Make the stock and leave it simmering on a low heat. Dice the onion and fry in the olive oil for about 5 minutes until soft. Add the sweet potato and the turmeric and fry for another 5 minutes on a medium heat, making sure not to burn the turmeric. Add the sweet potato and onion to the stock and bring to the boil. Cover and leave to simmer for 10 minutes on a low heat. Then mix everything with a hand blender until you have a smooth soup before adding the cream, mustard, and the orange juice. Season with salt and pepper and pour the soup into bowls. Garnish with the flat leaf parsley.

Soup whenever you feel like it

ROCKET SOUP

with chilli pepper

When you think of rocket you probably don't automatically think of all the great soups you can make from it. Indeed, you have probably never even heard of rocket soup before! Which is not strange, because the delicate rocket leaf is full of flavour and therefore usually used in salads in combination with a really good olive oil, freshly ground pepper and Parmesan cheese. That's it you might think, but nothing could be further from the truth because rocket undergoes a magical transformation when cooked with floury potatoes, chilli peppers and a good stock. After quick spin with the blender you'll have a superb soup; don't forget to top it with crisps, of course, as they really add that extra special finishing touch.

serves *4* | preparation time *20* minutes

1 litre vegetable stock (3 cubes)
3 tbsp olive oil for frying
1 onion, finely chopped
500 g floury potatoes, peeled and chopped
   into 1 cm cubes
2 cloves of garlic, finely chopped

2 chilli peppers, deseeded and finely chopped
300 g rocket salad leaves
½ tsp sea salt and black pepper
4 handfuls unsalted crisps

Make the stock and leave it on a low heat. Heat the olive oil in a large frying pan and fry the onion for 5 minutes until soft. Add the potato and the garlic and fry for another 5 minutes on a medium heat. Add this mixture, plus the chilli pepper, to the stock and bring to the boil. Leave to cook for 15 minutes, or until the potatoes are done. Add the rocket 30 seconds before the end, then remove the saucepan from the heat. Mix the soup until smooth with a hand blender and season to taste with salt and pepper. Scatter crisps on top just before serving.

Soup whenever you feel like it

TOMATO SOUP

with roasted peppers

During my first pregnancy, I went to live and work in Cologne in Germany for a few months. I stayed in a hotel and ate out a lot in all kinds of restaurants. After a while I knew exactly where to go when I wanted to eat a particular food. One of the things that I craved almost every day was tomatoes – morning, noon and night. They could be stuffed into a sandwich for lunch or piping hot in soup for dinner, it didn't matter so long as I got to eat enough – bizarre, to say the least. Later, I found out that tomatoes are very rich in vitamin C, an essential vitamin when you are pregnant, which explained a lot. Vitamin C helps to build strong bones and teeth, enables your body to process iron and assists with healing. Of course, I was still left wondering why I only wanted tomatoes? Why not oranges as well? I don't know the answer to this, but in the meantime, I have learned to trust my body and to listen to what it tells me it needs. The soup in this recipe is not only rich in vitamin C, but also delicious – and not just for pregnant women.

---

serves *4* | preparation time *20* minutes

---

2 large peppers
3 vegetable stock cubes
1½ kilo ripe tomatoes, quartered
1 clove of garlic, crushed
1 tbsp thyme
1 tbsp oregano

3 bay leaves
40 ml extra virgin olive oil
1 tsp sea salt and freshly ground black pepper
1 handful fresh basil, finely chopped

Preheat the oven to 200°C. Place the peppers in an oven dish or on a baking tray covered with baking paper and roast in the oven for 20 minutes until the skin starts to blacken. In the meantime, bring a large saucepan with 200 ml water to the boil and add the stock cubes and tomatoes. Then add the garlic, thyme, oregano and bay leaves. Cover and cook for 10 minutes. Take the peppers out of the oven, leave to cool for a few minutes. Peel, deseed and chop the peppers and add them to the soup. Pour in most of the olive oil (retain a little for later). Mix with a hand blender until smooth and season with salt and pepper. Pour the soup into bowls, garnish with the fresh basil and sprinkle with the leftover extra virgin olive oil.

Soup whenever you feel like it

PEA AND MINT SOUP

It is something of a miracle that my brother Niels and I are such enthusiastic cooks, given that I have never been able to identify the required skills in either of our parents. Nevertheless, Niels is a dab hand when it comes to soup and we love cooking the Christmas dinner together whenever we can. I remember very well that fateful summer's day when I was out walking in the woods with my kids and my mother and we ran into Niels and his friend 'Nicky', who is now my husband. Nicholas had a dog, Junior, with him (who is now very senior, and still our favourite and living with us here in Ibiza). For Nicholas and I it was love at first sight, which is probably why I can still remember the wonderful pea and mint soup that my brother made us for lunch that day.

serves *4* | preparation time *20* minutes

2 shallots
3 tbsp olive oil for frying
¼ litre dry, full-bodied white wine (for example, Chardonnay)
½ litre water
2 vegetable stock cubes
2 tbsp fresh thyme

1 kg peas (fresh or frozen)
1 large handful fresh mint leaves, plus extra for garnishing
1 tsp sea salt and freshly ground black pepper
125 ml crème fraîche
extra virgin olive oil
zest of ½ lemon for garnishing

Finely chop the shallots and fry in olive oil for 5–7 minutes until soft. Pour in the white wine and the water and add the stock cubes and the fresh thyme. Bring to the boil and then add the peas. Reduce the heat and cook for 1 minute. Remove from the heat, add the fresh mint and mix with a hand blender until smooth. Season with salt and pepper and pour the soup into bowls. Add a large tablespoon of crème fraîche to each serving and sprinkle with a little extra virgin olive oil, the lemon zest and some fresh mint.

Soup whenever you feel like it

Sweet
POTATO SOUP
with cannellini beans

Beans and sweet potato was a combination that I once tried out on a bleak winter's day and that, to my very great surprise, tuned out to be delicious. It wasn't just the taste that was perfect, but also the fabulous colours in the bowl. This soup is still a firm winter favourite in our house.

serves *4* | preparation time *20* minutes

1 litre vegetable stock (2 cubes)
1 medium-sized white onion, diced
1 clove of garlic, crushed
60 ml olive oil for frying
2 medium-sized sweet potatoes, peeled and
   chopped into small pieces
½ chilli pepper, deseeded and finely chopped
1½ tsp cumin powder

400 g cannellini beans (1 tin/jar), drained
15 g coriander, leaves only
50 g brown mushrooms, sliced
sea salt and freshly ground black pepper
extra virgin olive oil for garnishing
chilli flakes

Bring the stock to the boil. Heat the olive oil in a frying pan and fry the onion for about 5 minutes. Add the garlic and fry for another minute, add the sweet potato and fry for 5 more minutes. Add the chilli pepper and cumin and, fry briefly on a high heat and then add the onions and potatoes to the stock. Pour in the cannellini beans, cover and cook for 10 minutes on a low heat. In the meantime, fry the mushrooms in a teaspoon of olive oil and a pinch of salt until golden brown and put to one side. Add the fresh coriander to the soup and mix with a hand blender until smooth. Season to taste with salt and pepper. Pour the soup into bowls and top off with the mushrooms. Garnish with extra virgin olive oil and some chilli flakes.

Soup whenever you feel like it

Green winter
VEGETABLE SOUP
with caramelised onions

Unfortunately, it is not easy to find kale here in Ibiza. Apparently it has something to do with the lack of frost on the island. Kale grows best after it has had a night's frost and although it can get cold here, it never freezes. In any event, this soup lends itself to endless variations; if you can't find one of the ingredients, just replace it with something else green. However, you cannot leave out the caramelised onions, because they give the soup the extra punch that is always so welcome on a cold winter's day. And don't leave out the sherry either – almost goes without saying.

serves *6* | preparation time *25* minutes

1 large white onion
25 g butter
2 tbsp olive oil
1½ litres vegetable stock (3 cubes)
2 spring onions
1 bulb of fennel
2 heads of broccoli
300 g kale or spinach
1 large clove of garlic or 2 small ones, crushed

60 ml sherry
15 g fresh chives
1 handful fresh coriander
2 handfuls flat leaf parsley
juice of ½ lemon
freshly ground black pepper
extra virgin olive oil
chilli flakes (optional)
wholemeal bread

Chop the onion in half, then into thin half rings. Heat the butter and olive oil in a small saucepan, add the onion and cover with a lid. Leave them to caramelise on a low heat for 20 minutes, stirring occasionally. In the meantime, bring the vegetable stock to the boil. Wash and chop the rest of the vegetables and add them to the stock together with the garlic. Bring to the boil again, turn down the heat and cover and leave the soup to simmer for 20 minutes. Add the sherry and the fresh herbs 5 minutes before the end of cooking. Finally add the caramelised onion and mix the soup with a hand blender until smooth. Season to taste with salt and pepper and the lemon juice. Pour the soup into bowls, add a drop of good quality extra virgin olive oil and sprinkle in some chilli flakes if you like. Serve with wholemeal bread.

Soup whenever you feel like it

Tomato soup
WITH TURMERIC

When you have three kids, there's a high chance that at least one of them is sick at any given moment. And no matter where you live or how much sunshine you get, schools will always be a breeding ground for all kinds of ailments, so you invariably end up making regular trips to the pharmacy to keep your medicine cabinet stocked up. At least, that is what you would be inclined to think! However, after we were all floored by a flu that just didn't want to go away, and after trying every kind of cough syrup and vitamin supplement under the sun, I decided it was time for a different approach. Scouring the internet for information, I came upon a homemade antibiotic made from garlic, cinnamon, lemon, honey and, amazingly, turmeric. I duly brewed the concoction, made my daughter take it three times a day and then watched in utter amazement how she quickly got better before my very eyes – if only I had known this earlier. Since then I've been using turmeric whenever and wherever I can, and you'd be surprised how many recipes I've managed to squeeze it into. It gives this tomato soup a taste of the Orient and provides your immune system with an enormous boost.

serves *4* | preparation time *20* minutes

1 red onion
2 cloves of garlic
2 tbsp olive oil for frying
200 g cherry or mini roma tomatoes, halved
1 level tbsp turmeric powder
salt and pepper
800 g tin organic tomatoes (1 large tin or 2 small
   ones), peeled and chopped

½ cup water
1 vegetable stock cube
1 tbsp apple cider vinegar
handful of fresh basil
extra virgin olive oil for garnishing

Finely chop the onion and the garlic and fry for 5 minutes in the olive oil until soft (use a sauté pan if you have one). Add the chopped tomatoes and fry for another 2 minutes before adding the turmeric and a twist of salt and pepper and fry for 1 more minute. Then add the tinned tomatoes, the water and the stock cube. Bring to the boil, reduce the heat, cover and leave to simmer for 10 minutes. Remove from the heat, mix with a hand blender until you have a smooth soup, then stir in the apple cider vinegar. Garnish with fresh basil and sprinkle with extra virgin olive oil. This is delicious with wholemeal bread.

Soup whenever you feel like it

COURGETTE SOUP

with coriander and onion

When my mother first introduced us to her current partner, Pierre, we were so impressed by his culinary skills that we thought he was some kind of superman – a man who could not only cook really well, but who enjoyed it too. Later, he confessed to us that it had been the first time he had really tried his best in the kitchen. He said that the he fact that he had pulled it off was nothing short of a miracle. However, it was exactly what he had needed to get the ball rolling and since then he has been cooking up a storm every evening in the kitchen. My mother can consider herself very lucky indeed. One of Pierre's specialities is soup, including this one, which is as easy to make as it is delicious.

serves *6* | preparation time *25* minutes

1 litre vegetable stock (3 cubes)
3 medium-sized courgettes
1 large onion
1 chilli pepper, deseeded
4 tbsp olive oil for frying
2 cloves of garlic, crushed

2 large handfuls coriander
1 tsp sea salt and freshly ground black pepper
extra virgin olive oil
dash of (soya) cream (optional)

Make the stock and leave it on a low heat. Wash the courgettes and chop into small pieces. Dice the onion and chop the chilli pepper into thin rings or strips. Heat the olive oil in a large frying pan and add the onion. Fry for 5 minutes, add the courgette and cook for another 5 minutes. Then add the onions, courgettes, pepper and garlic to the stock, bring it to the boil, simmer for 10 minutes, then remove from the heat. Add the coriander to the soup and mix with a hand blender until smooth. Season with salt and pepper. Pour the soup into bowls and add a dash of (soya) cream if using. Finish with a few drops of good quality extra virgin olive oil and serve with bread.

Soup whenever you feel like it

DRESSINGS

Classic vinaigrette
60 ml lemon juice
60 ml red wine vinegar
40 ml extra virgin olive oil
1 tsp mustard
2 tsp honey
½ tsp sea salt and freshly ground black pepper

Mustard dressing
60 ml extra virgin olive oil
juice of ½ lemon
1 large tsp mayonnaise
1 tsp Dijon mustard
1 tsp coarse-grain mustard
1 tsp honey
½ tsp Himalayan or sea salt
lots of freshly ground black pepper
1 clove of garlic, crushed

Green goddess dressing
1 ripe avocado, in small pieces
1 bunch chives, finely chopped
2 tbsp flat leaf parsley, finely chopped
1 tbsp fresh or dried tarragon, finely chopped
¼ cup apple cider vinegar
2 tbsp lemon juice
1 clove of garlic, crushed
sea salt and freshly ground black pepper
1 tsp honey

Caesar dressing
2 tbsp organic mayonnaise
2 tsp Dijon mustard
juice of ½ lime
3 tbsp extra virgin olive oil
½ clove of garlic, crushed

Tahini dressing

½ clove of garlic, crushed
coarse sea salt
2 tbsp light tahini
zest and juice of ½ lemon
juice of ½ orange
½ tsp honey
freshly ground black pepper
2 tbsp extra virgin olive oil

Soya and sambal oelek (chilli paste) dressing

100 ml extra virgin olive oil
4 tbsp soya sauce
2 heaped tsp Dijon mustard
2 heaped tsp sambal oelek
2 tbsp mayonnaise
freshly ground black pepper

Rosemary vinaigrette

60 ml olive oil
2 tbsp dried rosemary
2 tbsp apple cider vinegar
½ tsp sea salt and freshly ground black pepper
1½ tsp honey

Avocado-coriander dressing

½ avocado, in small pieces
¼ cup Greek yoghurt
1 cup coriander leaves, finely chopped
1 clove of garlic, crushed
½ tsp salt
juice of ½ lime

Warm caper dressing

2 tbsp capers
juice of 1 lemon
60 ml olive oil
½ tsp sea salt
freshly ground black pepper

Hummus*

400 g chickpeas (plus a little cooking liquid)
juice of 1 lemon
2 tbsp tahini
4 tbsp extra virgin olive oil
1 clove of garlic, crushed
sea salt and freshly ground black pepper

Black bean tapenade with cumin

300 g drained black beans from a tin/jar
60 ml extra virgin olive oil
½ tsp cumin powder
sea salt and freshly ground black pepper to taste

Mix with a hand blender until you
have a smooth paste.

Basil pesto

40 g basil
40 g Parmesan cheese, grated
1 clove of garlic, crushed
120 ml extra virgin olive oil
40 g pine nuts
½ tsp sea salt and freshly ground black pepper

Mix everything with a hand blender.

Mexican salsa

3 tomatoes, peeled and chopped
½ cucumber, peeled and chopped
1 handful fresh coriander, finely chopped
½ red onion, diced
2 tbsp olive oil
sea salt and freshly ground black pepper

Mix everything together.

Parsley pesto

40 g fresh flat leaf parsley, finely chopped
40 g Parmesan cheese, grated
1 clove of garlic, crushed
120 ml extra virgin olive oil
1 lemon, the zest and half of the juice
½ tsp sea salt and freshly ground black pepper
Mix everything with a hand blender.

Nan's dip

4 large heaped tbsp organic
mayonnaise
2 large heaped tbsp crème
fraîche
2 tbsp chives, finely chopped
½ tsp salt
½ tsp freshly ground black
pepper
1 clove of garlic, crushed

Mix everything together well.

Soya dip with onions

6 tbsp soya sauce
1 tbsp sesame oil
¼ red onion, diced
3 tbsp rice vinegar
2 tsp honey
2 tbsp chilli sauce
freshly ground black pepper
Mix everything together
thoroughly in a sealed jar.

Olive tapenade

300 g deseeded black olives from a tin/jar
30 g Parmesan cheese
1 clove of garlic
80 ml extra virgin olive oil
freshly ground black pepper

Mix with a hand blender until you have a smooth paste.

Coriander hummus*

400 g chickpeas (plus a little cooking liquid)
juice of 1 lemon
2 tbsp tahini
4 tbsp extra virgin olive oil
1 clove of garlic, crushed
sea salt and freshly ground black pepper
1 large handful fresh coriander

DIPS

* For the chickpea-based dips use a food processor to 'mash' them. If the resulting mixture is too thick, add a little cooking liquid and continue blending until you have achieved the desired consistency. For the coriander version, add the coriander when blending. Season the hummus by adding lemon juice, tahini, garlic, pepper and salt. Only add the olive oil at the very end.

LASAGNE

with spinach and crème fraîche

There is not much more I can say about this lasagne other than it is just divine. It may not be exactly calorie-free, thanks to the cheese and crème fraîche, but believe me it will earn you loads of brownie points. This dish is not only simple, but delicious too – so get cooking.

serves *4-5* | preparation time *40* minutes

4–5 tbsp olive oil for frying
1 large white onion, finely chopped
3 stalks of celery, chopped
2 cloves of garlic, finely chopped
250 g mushrooms, chopped
1 courgette, chopped
250 g fresh spinach
800 g chopped tomatoes (from a jar/tin),
2 tbsp thyme
1 tbsp oregano

1 vegetable stock cube
125 ml dry white wine
sea salt and freshly ground black pepper
1 pack lasagne sheets, white or green
125 ml crème fraîche
150 g mature cheese, grated
2–3 fresh tomatoes, sliced
1 handful Parmesan cheese

Preheat the oven to 180°C. Prepare all of the vegetables. Heat the olive oil in a sauté or frying pan and fry the onion for 5 minutes until soft. Add the celery and fry for another few minutes. Then add the garlic, mushrooms and courgette and continue frying for another 5–7 minutes before adding the spinach and allowing it to shrink. Add the tomatoes and then the thyme, oregano, stock cube and the white wine. Bring to the boil, cover and leave the sauce to simmer for a while on a low heat. Season with salt and pepper. Take a rectangular oven dish and pour in a layer of sauce. Cover with a layer of lasagne sheets. Then add a thin layer of crème fraîche and half of the grated cheese. Repeat one more time. Finish off with a layer of sauce, the tomato slices and the grated Parmesan cheese. Put the lasagne in the oven and bake for 20–25 minutes. To check whether the lasagne sheets are cooked, prick them with a fork.

CHILLI

with orange and cumin

Chilli is a typical winter dish, but to be honest I love making it in the summer as well. Beans are one of my favourite ingredients after all. They are great for combining with other stuff and incredibly nutritious, not to mention rich in proteins and fibre and full of important minerals like iron, phosphorus and magnesium. Beans also help to control your blood sugar and cholesterol levels and are very good for your heart. So, unless you cannot stand the taste of beans, there is no reason not to eat them. This vegetarian version of chilli con carne is superb not only as a result of the spices in it (especially cumin and cinnamon), but also because the juice and zest of the orange have been added. That may seem a weird combination (and it is), but it is delicious.

serves *4-5* | preparation time *30* minutes

300 g (wholegrain) basmati rice
1 orange
4 tbsp olive oil for frying (or refined coconut oil)
2 large white onions, finely chopped
4 cloves of garlic, crushed
4 tsp chilli powder (or less, depending on your taste)
4 tsp cumin powder
4 tsp cinnamon powder

800 g black beans, drained
400 g kidney beans, drained
800 g chopped tomatoes (from a jar/tin)
sea salt and freshly ground black pepper
125 ml crème fraîche or Greek yoghurt
2 large handfuls coriander, leaves only
tabasco sauce (optional)

Cook the rice according to the instructions with 1 teaspoon of salt. Drain and leave to continue steaming with the lid on. Wash the orange, grate the zest very finely and squeeze out the juice. Set aside. Heat the oil in a saucepan with a heavy base and fry the onions for about 5 minutes on a medium heat. Add the garlic and the spices. Stir well before adding the beans, the tomatoes and half of the orange juice. Season with salt and pepper. Bring to the boil, reduce the heat and leave to simmer for 15 minutes so that the flavours can blend; stir at regular intervals to make sure that nothing sticks to the bottom. Add the rest of the orange juice and the zest and leave to simmer for a few more minutes, then serve the chilli in bowls with the rice. Top each serving with a large spoon of crème fraîche or Greek yoghurt, sprinkle with lots of coriander and add a drop of tabasco sauce if you like.

FAROTTO

Although I'm a big fan of 'ordinary' risotto, I much prefer farotto. Farro is a member of the spelt family, but it is not quite the same and people often confuse them. The great advantage of farro is that it cooks in around 45 minutes, whereas spelt can take hours. The latter is not a problem when you can leave your spelt cooking all day while attending to other things, before eventually using it in a salad or whatever, but it is not exactly handy when you want a quick risotto-like supper. Like a risotto, when making farotto, you can use whatever fresh ingredients you like and you don't even have to stick to the ones listed I've suggested. For example, you could try mushrooms with truffle or peas with spinach and lime, there is no end to the possibilities. In the meantime, this recipe is well worth a try.

serves *4* | preparation time *40* minutes

1 leek, sliced into rings
50 g butter, halved
4 tbsp olive oil for frying
1½ litres vegetable stock (3 cubes)
1 onion, finely chopped
1 clove of garlic, finely chopped
1 tsp dried of fresh thyme
300 g farro
250 ml white wine

150 g kale, finely chopped (leaves only)
50 g grated Parmesan cheese, plus extra for
  on the side
sea salt and freshly ground black pepper
1 tbsp chilli flakes
extra virgin olive oil for garnishing
50 g soft goat's cheese

First, fry the leek in a frying pan with half of the butter and half of the olive oil until it starts to brown slightly and then sprinkle with a little salt and pepper and set aside. Make the stock and leave it simmering on a low heat. Heat the rest of the butter and the olive oil in a large saucepan with a heavy base and add the onion. Fry for 5 minutes before adding the garlic and thyme. Fry for a few more minutes until the onion starts to brown. Add the farro and stir-fry for 2 minutes until all of the grains are covered with butter and oil. Pour in the wine and bring to the boil. Reduce the heat and allow the farro to soak up the wine. Then add just enough stock to cover the farro. Keep stirring and add more stock when the farotto starts to become drier. After 15 minutes, add the kale to the farotto and cook for another 10 minutes until the farro is done. Stir in the leek and the Parmesan cheese and season with salt and pepper. Spoon the farotto onto plates, top with goat's cheese, sprinkle with a few chilli flakes and drizzle with a little extra virgin olive oil. Serve with the extra parmesan on the side.

In the evening

Sarah's
BURNT BROCCOLI
pasta

Nicholas was in the Netherlands when Sarah and Ben first invited me and the kids to come over for dinner. We got to know one another through the children's school and had immediately become good friends. They live in the village at the foot of the mountain, where a twisting and bumpy little road takes you passed an orchard and up to their wonderful house. I arrived late (as usual, to quote Sarah) and I remember thinking that something wasn't quite right when I walked into the kitchen. Maybe the dinner was ruined because I had turned up way too late. I handed Sarah the bottle of wine I had brought along and peeked over her shoulder to see what was burning in the frying pan on the stove. She must have noticed the worried look on my face because she immediately said: 'Oh, don't worry! That's the way it's supposed to be – it's called burnt broccoli and it's amazing!' I had my doubts. In my kitchen, it was not a good idea to burn food, but who was I to interfere – we had been invited over for dinner after all. The broccoli turned out to be absolutely delicious. So, when Nicholas came home it was the first thing I made for him. 'Never mind the burnt bits. They're supposed to be like that' I assured him. I can still see the look of deep suspicion on his face.

serves *4*	preparation time *20* minutes

4 tbsp olive oil for frying
2 large heads of broccoli, cut into small florets, and the stem peeled and sliced
sea salt and freshly ground black pepper
500 g spaghetti or linguine

40 g pine nuts
extra virgin olive oil
4 dried small chilli peppers, finely chopped
50 g Parmesan cheese, grated

Heat the olive oil in a large frying pan (with a heavy base) and fry the broccoli until it starts to brown, and then keep on frying! You don't need to burn it to a cinder (not healthy), just make sure the edges are well browned and a little bit crispy. Season with salt and pepper. In the meantime, bring a saucepan of water with salt to the boil and cook the pasta according to the instructions on the packaging. Roast the pine nuts in a dry frying pan on a medium heat; stir continuously as pine nuts burn very easily. Drain the pasta, stir in some extra virgin olive oil to stop it from sticking and spoon it out onto your prettiest plates. Divide the broccoli between the plates before topping off with the chilli peppers, pine nuts and lots of Parmesan cheese.

In the evening

SPINACH CASSEROLE
with chickpeas and poached eggs

I love the one-pot meal concept because it is so practical and convenient, and I resort to it whenever I can. My days are usually busy enough and the last thing I need is to have to clean away a huge pile of pots and pans after the rest of the family has gulped down the fruits of my labour in the kitchen in less than five minutes. Somehow or other it is always me who ends having to do these things (cooking is no problem, but all the cleaning up afterwards too...). Strangely enough I still haven't been able to light the fires of enthusiasm in my kids for these chores either. The idea that they could lend a helping hand hasn't sunk in yet it seems, so all I can do is make things as easy as possible for myself. Everything into the one pot, and while that bubbles away on the stove I can put the stuff I don't need any more into the dishwasher before it's time to eat. Sounds easy, doesn't it? I often wish my children thought the same way...

---

serves *4* | preparation time *40* minutes

---

2 medium-sized onions, finely chopped
2 cloves of garlic, finely chopped
8 tbsp olive oil
250 g mushrooms, sliced
400 g spinach
400 g chickpeas (from a jar/tin)
400 g tomatoes (from a jar/tin), chopped
1½ tsp chilli powder

2 tbsp dried thyme
1½ tsp cumin powder
100 ml (soya) cream for cooking
2 handfuls fresh flat leaf parsley, finely chopped,
    plus extra for garnishing
6 eggs
salt and freshly ground black pepper

Heat 4 tablespoons of olive oil in a large flat saucepan and fry the onion and garlic for about 5 minutes until they start to brown. Put the mushrooms in the pan and fry for another 5 minutes. Add the remaining olive oil, throw in the spinach and allow it to shrink, stirring continuously. Then add the chickpeas and tomatoes, followed by the chilli powder, thyme and cumin powder. Pour in the cream, stir well and season with salt and pepper. Toss in 1 handful of parsley and then use a spoon to make little 'potholes' into which you can break the eggs (be careful not to break the yokes). Season to taste with a little salt and pepper, cover and allow to simmer on a low heat for about 15 minutes. Add another handful of parsley and serve (with rice or bread, too, if you like).

In the evening

FRIES!

Fries made from sweet potato are delicious and easy to make; you don't even need to peel the potatoes. Chop them into strips about 1-cm thick, toss them in olive oil then bake in the oven for about 20 minutes at 180°C. Sprinkle them with sea salt and whatever fresh herbs you fancy and serve with 'Nan's dip' (see p.95).

RIGATONI
with capers and mint

This is an old family favourite. So much so that the kids have long since dropped the 'rigatoni' and refer to it simply as 'capers and mint'. Everyone in our family loves it and it's a great dish to fall back on whenever I'm caught for time or feeling uninspired. It is tasty and refreshing; somehow pasta always seems to hit the spot.

serves *4* | preparation time *20* minutes

500 g rigatoni or penne
1 large onion, finely chopped
4 tbsp olive oil for frying
2 cloves of garlic, finely chopped
800 g tomatoes (from a jar/tin)
125 ml (soya) cream

50 g capers
2 handfuls fresh mint, large and small leaves
  separated
1 tsp sea salt and freshly ground black pepper
Parmesan cheese, grated

Bring a saucepan of water to the boil, add a pinch of salt and cook the pasta according to the instructions on the packaging. In the meantime, heat the olive oil in a frying pan with a heavy base, add the onion and fry for about 5 minutes on a medium heat before adding the garlic. Continue frying for a few more minutes until the onion is soft and slightly browned. Add the tomatoes and the cream and bring to the boil. Turn down the heat, cover and leave to simmer for a few minutes. Drain the capers and add them to the sauce. Leave to simmer for another 5 minutes. Season with salt and pepper. Stir the sauce into the pasta and then add the large mint leaves. Garnish with the small mint leaves, sprinkle with the Parmesan cheese and serve.

In the evening

Real
RATATOUILLE

When I went with my kids to see the film Ratatouille, I was spellbound. The film was very enjoyable, of course, but it was the ratatouille itself that really grabbed me, even though it was only a cartoon – I simply had to make it. After some detective work, and three failed attempts, I finally came up with a fabulous ratatouille with tomato, courgette and aubergine, all thinly sliced and baked in a tomato and pepper sauce. When served with homemade celeriac mash you have a wonderfully light meal (unless you help yourself to more and more of course). In any event, according to my children, this ratatouille is the genuine article – and that's saying something.

serves *4* | preparation time *80* minutes

Tomato-pepper sauce
2 red peppers, deseeded and chopped
2 large or 3 small onions, diced
2 cloves of garlic, finely chopped
3 tbsp olive oil for frying
400 g tomatoes (fresh or from a jar/tin)
sea salt and freshly ground black pepper
1½ tbsp dried thyme

Vegetables
Pick vegetables that are all roughly the same diameter so that the slices fit neatly next to each other.
1 courgette
1 aubergine
4–5 tomatoes

Topping
60 ml olive oil
2 cloves of garlic, finely chopped
2 tbsp fresh thyme, finely chopped
2 tbsp fresh oregano, finely chopped
½ tsp sea salt and freshly ground black pepper
1 handful fresh sprigs of thyme and oregano

Mashed celeriac
1 medium-sized celeriac
50 ml (soya) cream
½ tsp sea salt and freshly ground black pepper
1 knob of butter

Preheat the oven to 180°C. First, make the sauce. Heat the oil in a frying pan and fry the onions for about 5 minutes until soft. Add the garlic and fry for 2 more minutes. Add the peppers and fry until they begin to soften and brown a little at the edges. Then add the tomatoes and thyme and season with salt and pepper. The sauce should have plenty of punch, so let it simmer for another 5 minutes. Purée the sauce with a hand blender until smooth and pour it into an 20–24 cm oven dish. Slice the aubergine, courgette and tomatoes into equal-sized pieces and arrange them alternately in rows on the sauce until the oven dish is completely full. Prepare the topping: mix the olive oil with the garlic and herbs (you don't have to stick rigidly to the list above), season with salt and pepper and pour it over the vegetables. Top the dish off with a few sprigs of thyme and oregano. Cover tightly with aluminium foil and bake the ratatouille for 1 hour in the middle of the oven. In the meantime, make the mash. Peel and chop the celeriac, then cook for about 20 minutes in plenty of water until done. Drain, add the cream, salt, pepper and butter and mix with a hand blender until smooth and creamy. Serve with the ratatouille.

In the evening

LENTIL CURRY

with cauliflower and sweet potato

Lentils, what's not to like about them? I'd run a mile for a good lentil recipe any day and a lentil curry had been on my list of things-to-make for a long time. This one requires the use of a lot of herbs and spices, but believe me, homemade is so much better than out of a jar. My husband would never even look at a lentil until the day I popped this curry in front of him... so it's never too late.

| serves *4* | preparation time *35* minutes |

300 g wholegrain rice
200 g brown lentils
2 tbsp olive oil for frying
1 sweet potato, in small pieces (approx. 200 g)
350 g cauliflower, in florets
1 red onion, chopped
2 cloves of garlic, crushed
2 cm fresh ginger, very finely chopped (about 10 g)
½ tsp coriander powder
600 ml coconut milk (1½ tins)

2 tsp garam masala
1 tsp turmeric powder
1 tsp cumin powder
¼ tsp cayenne pepper
150 g peas (fresh or frozen)
1 tsp sea salt and freshly ground black pepper
juice of 1 lime
1 lime, quartered
1 large handful fresh coriander
Greek yoghurt or crème fraîche

Cook the rice according to the instructions. Drain when done, cover and set aside. Cook the lentils according to the instructions on the packaging, but do not add any salt, otherwise whey will fall apart on you! Set aside when done. Heat the olive oil in a frying pan with a heavy base and fry the onion for about 5 minutes. Then add the garlic, ginger and coriander powder and fry for another 2 minutes. Add the cauliflower and sweet potato along with 50 ml water, cover and cook for 7 minutes on a low heat, or until done. Then add the coconut milk and the rest of the spices – garam masala, turmeric, cumin and cayenne pepper. Stir well, cover and leave to simmer on a low heat for 5 minutes. Add the peas and the lentils and cook for another 5 minutes on a low heat to allow the spices to blend with each other. Finally, season with salt and pepper and stir in the lime juice. Serve the curry with lime quarters, fresh coriander, Greek yoghurt or crème fraîche and wholegrain rice.

In the evening

Warm tri-colour
BEAN SALAD

Beans – darlings one and all, regardless of their colour, shape or size. I wouldn't think twice about buying a can of black beans and eating them on the spot. The rest of my family, however, is a little less enthusiastic about them and will only eat beans if they are accompanied by other ingredients, which is fair enough. This recipe is not only superb in terms of taste, but also because of its blaze of colour. It is great as a side dish, or as a main when served with rice or quinoa.

serves *3-4* | preparation time *25* minutes

150 g French beans
150 g white beans (from a jar/tin), drained
300 g broad beans (preferably fresh, but frozen
   will do)
½ red onion, in thin rings
1 handful flat leaf parsley, chopped
4 tbsp extra virgin olive oil
2 tsp coriander powder

1½ tsp mustard seeds, lightly crushed in pestle &
   mortar
1 tsp chilli flakes
zest of 1 lemon, and some of the juice for sprinkling
1 clove of garlic, very finely chopped
sea salt and freshly ground black pepper

Wash the French beans, trim off the ends and cook for 5–7 minutes in water with a pinch of salt. Drain and dunk in a bowl of ice-cold water briefly so that they retain their green colour, then drain again. Cook the broad beans for 1 minute, drain and, using a sharp knife, cut an opening in the outer skin until you can pop the bean out. Put all the beans into a large bowl along with the onion and the parsley. Fry the mustard seeds in olive oil until they start to pop, turn down the heat and add the coriander powder and the chilli flakes. Fry for another 30 seconds and then stir the mixture into the beans. Add the lemon zest and garlic and season with salt and pepper. Finally, sprinkle with a little lemon juice.

In the evening

RISOTTO
with green spring vegetables

This book would not be complete without a recipe for risotto. At first I wasn't sure whether to include instructions on how to make the risotto rice itself, but I decided that it is impossible to make a good risotto until you have mastered the basics. The fact of the matter is that there are a few tips and tricks that you simply need to know if you want your risotto to be perfect – and believe me, they are worth learning. Once you have mastered the basic recipe, the possibilities are endless. So here is my basic risotto recipe followed by the recipe for one of my favourite spring vegetable risotto.

serves *3-4* | preparation time *40* minutes

Basic risotto
1½ litre vegetable stock (3 cubes)
1 large onion, chopped very finely
40 g butter
4 tbsp olive oil for frying
300 g arborio rice or other risotto rice
200 ml dry white wine (for example, Chardonnay)
100 g Parmesan cheese, grated
sea salt and freshly ground black pepper

Spring vegetables
1 bunch green asparagus, ends trimmed off
   and chopped in 1½ cm pieces
1 tbsp dried thyme
1 tbsp dried oregano
150 g (baby) spinach
150 g peas
1 lemon, the zest and half of the juice
extra Parmesan cheese, grated
extra virgin olive oil

First, the basic recipe. Make the stock and leave to simmer next to the pan in which you will be making the risotto. Heat the olive oil and half of the butter in a large frying pan with a heavy base and fry the onion until soft. After 5 minutes add the rice and fry for another 2 minutes until the rice and the oil have mixed well. Stirring continuously, add the wine and allow it to be absorbed completely by the rice. Then add just enough stock to cover the rice and keep stirring until it has been (almost) completely absorbed, and then add some more stock. Keep doing this until all the stock has been used up or until the rice is done (don't let it get too mushy). Take the risotto off the heat, stir in the Parmesan cheese and the rest of the butter and season with salt and pepper.

For the risotto with spring vegetables, first make the risotto by following the instructions above up to the point where you have been cooking the stock and the rice for about 20 minutes, then add the asparagus, thyme and oregano. Cook for 5 minutes before adding the spinach. When the spinach has shrunk, add the peas and the lemon juice (keep stirring all the time). When the rice is done, add the Parmesan cheese and the rest of the butter. Season with salt and pepper. Spoon the risotto onto plates, garnish with a little extra Parmesan cheese and the lemon zest and drizzle with extra virgin olive oil.

WHOLEMEAL PIZZA

three variations

You may not know this, but a pizza can be pretty healthy. The trick is to leave out all of the 'white' stuff that does little more than make you fat, and use wholemeal products and fresh vegetables instead. Without trying to make you jealous, I have to tell you that when we came to live in Ibiza one of the first things we found in our new back garden was an original stone oven. The first time my brother came to stay with us, it officially became our pizza oven. Believe me, I have never made so many pizzas in my life. Below you'll find my basic pizza dough recipe and on the following pages, three of our favourite pizza toppings.

for *8* pizzas │ preparation time *2* hours and *25* minutes (incl. resting and rising)

Basic pizza dough
100 ml warm water
10 g dry yeast
1 tsp sugar
700 g wholemeal flour (or white flour if you prefer)

2 tsp sea salt
1 tbsp olive oil
300 ml lukewarm water

Mix 100 ml water, the dry yeast and the sugar in a glass and leave to rest for 10 minutes. Pour the flour into a large bowl. Make a small hollow in the middle of the flour and add the salt, the olive oil and the lukewarm water. Add the yeast mix (after it has rested for 10 minutes) and mix well with the flour until the resulting dough no longer sticks to the sides of the bowl. Place on a clean surface and knead for about 10 minutes until you have a supple ball of dough. Return it to the bowl, cover with a damp tea towel and leave to rise for 1 hour until it has doubled in size. Carefully remove the ball of dough from the bowl and cut it into 8 portions, like you would cut a cake. Brush the portions with olive oil and roll each one into a ball, but don't knead them as the dough must remain as light as possible. Cover each 'ball' with cling film and leave to rest for 1 hour. Without using a rolling pin, try to press the balls down as best you can into nice flat circles – the bigger the circle, the thinner the pizza. Then, using your finger, make a groove measuring about 1 cm from the edge; this forms the crust. You can then top the dough using whatever ingredients you like. Bake your pizzas for 7 to 10 minutes in a (pizza) oven preheated to 200°C. If you have any dough left over, wrap it in cling film and put it in the freezer (it will keep for up to a month).

In the evening

Pizza with
LENTILS
and lots of greens

for *1* pizza

60 ml tomato pizza topping
40 g mature cheese, grated
¼ courgette, very thinly sliced
50 g cooked lentils, drained
1 tbsp dried oregano

¼ red onion, sliced into very thin rings
sea salt and freshly ground black pepper
2 tbsp extra virgin olive oil
1 handful rocket salad leaves for garnishing
1 handful fresh basil

Preheat the oven to 200°C. Using the back of a tablespoon, spread the tomato sauce over the pizza base up to the groove around the edge. Then add the cheese, courgette, lentils, oregano and onion and sprinkle with a tablespoon of olive oil. Season with salt and pepper. Bake the pizza for 7–10 minutes in an oven. Garnish with the rocket leaves and the basil and sprinkle with remaining olive oil.

In the evening

Pizza with
RICOTTA AND BROCCOLI

for *1* pizza

60 ml tomato pizza topping
40 g mature cheese, grated
125 g ricotta (½ tub)
sea salt and freshly ground black pepper
1 tsp dried oregano
100 g broccoli florets, sliced

¼ red onion, in thin rings
4 tbsp parsley pesto (see p.25)
2 tbsp extra virgin olive oil
½ handful fresh basil or flat leaf parsley
1 tbsp lemon zest for garnishing

Preheat the oven to 200°C. Mix the ricotta with the oregano and ½ teaspoon of salt and pepper. Using the back of a tablespoon, spread the tomato sauce over the pizza base up to the groove around the edge. Then add the cheese, the ricotta mix, broccoli, onion and parsley pesto. Sprinkle with a tablespoon of olive oil and salt and pepper. Bake the pizza for 7–10 minutes. Garnish with the basil or parsley, lemon zest and a tablespoon of olive oil.

Pizza
FUNGI
with parsley and truffle cream

for *1* pizza

40 ml tomato pizza topping
50 g mature cheese, grated
2 tbsp olive oil for frying
1 small onion, diced
1 clove of garlic, finely chopped
250 g mushrooms, very finely chopped

2 handfuls flat leaf parsley, finely chopped
50 ml (soya) cream
2 tbsp truffle oil
sea salt and freshly ground black pepper
1 handful rocket salad leaves for garnishing
fresh flat leaf parsley for garnishing

Preheat the oven to 200°C. Fry the onion in the olive oil for 5 minutes until soft, add the garlic and fry for one more minute. Add the mushrooms and parsley and fry until the mushrooms have browned slightly. Season with salt and pepper. To make the truffle cream, mix the cream with the truffle oil, ¼ teaspoon of salt and a generous twist of pepper. Using the back of a tablespoon, spread the tomato sauce over the pizza base up to the groove around the edge. Then add the grated cheese and the mushroom-parsley mixture. Sprinkle with the truffle cream. Bake the pizza for 7 to 10 minutes. Garnish with the rocket and parsley.

In the evening

Easy
QUINOA
with griddled fennel with honey and pomegranate seeds

If you like quinoa as much as I do, then you have probably already found hundreds of ways to include it in your daily meals. What is more, you may have even managed to do so for days on end without your family even knowing that they have been eating it. I'll say it again – quinoa is a fantastic product, and even though it is usually eaten as a grain (like rice) it is in fact a seed of South American origin. These days, due to the huge demand, quinoa is also grown in Europe, which is just as well, because it keeps the price from going through the roof and ensures that the farmers growing the original product have enough to feed their local population too.

serves *2-3* | preparation time *25* minutes

300 g quinoa
½ tsp salt
1 fennel bulb
3 tbsp olive oil for frying
2 tbsp dried thyme
3 tbsp organic honey

2 tbsp extra virgin olive oil
100 g pomegranate seeds
fresh sprigs of thyme for garnishing
sea salt and freshly ground black pepper
chilli flakes (optional)

Wash the quinoa thoroughly and cook it 2 parts water to 1 part quinoa and a ½ teaspoon of salt for 12–14 minutes until the white dots on the grains have disappeared. Drain, cover and set aside. Slice the fennel lengthways into 7 mm slices. Heat the olive oil in a griddle pan and cook the fennel slices on both sides for about 4 minutes until they start to brown – throw in the sprigs of thyme, too. Remove from the heat, add the honey and toss. Season with salt and pepper. Stir 2 tablespoons of olive oil into the quinoa, season with salt and pepper and dish it out on to the plates. Place the fennel slices on top and garnish with the pomegranate seeds and a sprinkling of chilli flakes if using.

In the evening

Stuffed
TOMATOES

with ricotta and parsnip mash

Some ingredients just beg to be combined with each other and you instinctively know that they will taste great together. Ricotta and tomato is one of these combinations– add a pinch of thyme and oregano and hey presto.

serves *4* | preparation time *35* minutes

Stuffed tomatoes
8 medium-sized tomatoes
500 g ricotta
2 tbsp dried thyme
1 tbsp dried oregano
1 tsp sea salt and freshly ground black pepper
1 tbsp lemon zest
40 g Parmesan cheese, grated
a few sprigs of fresh thyme for garnishing

Tomato sauce
1 medium-sized onion, diced
2 tbsp olive oil for frying
2 cloves of garlic, finely chopped

1 tbsp dried thyme
800 g tomatoes (from a jar/tin)
1 tsp sea salt and freshly ground black pepper
100 ml (soya) cream

Parsnip mash
500 g parsnip
1 clove of garlic, crushed
100 ml (soya) cream
1 tbsp dried thyme
25 g butter
sea salt and freshly ground black pepper

Preheat the oven to 180°C. Slice the top off each tomato and spoon out the flesh (which you will use to make the sauce). Make the sauce: fry the onion in the olive oil for about 5 minutes until it starts to brown, add the garlic and thyme and fry for another minute. Finally add the tinned tomatoes, the flesh you scooped out of the fresh tomatoes, salt, pepper and the cream. Cover and leave the sauce to simmer for 5 minutes on a low heat. In the meantime, make the stuffing by mixing the ricotta, thyme, oregano, salt, pepper, lemon zest and Parmesan cheese. Spoon the stuffing into the tomatoes. Pour the sauce into a large oven dish and arrange the tomatoes neatly on top. Garnish with the sprigs of fresh thyme and bake for 20 minutes in the oven. Make the mash. Peel and chop the parsnip and cook it in plenty of water with a pinch of salt for about 4 minutes until done. Mash the cooked parsnip with the cream, thyme, garlic, butter and salt and pepper until smooth. Serve with the stuffed tomatoes.

In the evening

'PIMIENTOS PADRON'

—

'Pimientos Padron' are Spanish peppers that are usually quite mild in terms of taste. They are fried for a few minutes in olive oil on a very high heat and served with coarse sea salt. They're delicious with a drink.

ROASTED PEPPER

curry

I fear I will never be able to make the perfect Indian butter chicken (it would have to be without chicken for me anyway), but I can live with that. The best Indian restaurant in the Netherlands by the way – no, scrap that, in the world – is situated in the village where I was born. I love Indian cuisine and have eaten saags, naans and curries all over the world, but none are as good as those served up at the Taj Mahal in Bussum (and no, they are not paying me to write this – although, while I'm at it, I recommend you pay a visit if you can). Anyway, one thing I have managed to perfect is this fantastic roast pepper curry. It might not have anything to do with the Taj Mahal, but that doesn't make it any less delicious.

serves *4* | preparation time *40* minutes

400 g basmati rice
2 large red peppers
5 tbsp olive oil
1 red onion, very finely chopped
3 cloves of garlic, finely chopped
1 tsp sea salt and freshly ground black pepper,
    plus extra for seasoning
400 ml coconut milk
400 g tomatoes (from a jar/tin)
4 large tbsp nutritional yeast flakes

2 tbsp cornflour
1 tsp chilli powder
1 tsp ginger powder
1 tsp coriander powder
2 tsp turmeric
400 g chickpeas (from a jar/tin), drained
150 g spinach
150 g cherry tomatoes, halved
fresh coriander

Preheat the oven to 220 °C. Cook the rice according to the instructions on the packaging, cover and set aside. Wash and dry the peppers, put them in an oven dish and bake for about 30 minutes until the skin starts to blacken. Remove from the oven, peel off the skins, remove the stalks and seeds and set aside. In the meantime, fry the onion for 5 minutes in the olive oil until soft and slightly browned. Add the garlic and fry for 1 more minute. Season with salt and pepper. Add the coconut milk, tinned tomatoes, nutritional yeast flakes, cornflour, chilli, ginger, coriander, turmeric and the roasted peppers. Mix with a hand blender until you have a smooth sauce; taste to see if it needs more salt and pepper. Transfer the sauce to a saucepan, add the spinach, chickpeas and cherry tomatoes, cover and leave to simmer for 15 minutes on a low heat. Serve the curry with the basmati rice and garnish with fresh coriander.

In the evening

Griddled
ARTICHOKES

I was out shopping one day at the local market when I spotted a basket full to the brim with small artichokes. I simply had to have them. My daughter loves them the classic way – served with a mustard sauce – but I was keen to try something different. So, I cut them in half and cooked them on a griddle pan with olive oil, garlic and lemon. They not only tasted fantastic, but they looked great too.

serves *4-8* | preparation time *20* minutes

4 small artichokes
100 ml olive oil for frying
3 cloves of garlic, crushed
2 handfuls flat leaf parsley, very finely chopped
1½ tsp sea salt and freshly ground black pepper
zest and juice of 1 lemon

Cook the artichokes whole in a saucepan with plenty of boiling water and half of the lemon juice. In the meantime, mix the olive oil with the garlic, parsley, salt, pepper, lemon zest and the rest of the lemon juice. Drain the cooked artichokes then slice them in half and brush them with the oil and lemon mixture. Heat a griddle pan and cook the artichokes on both sides for 5–7 minutes until they start to brown (the exact cooking time depends on the size of the artichokes).

In the evening

Veggie
PAELLA
olé!

In Spain, paella is part of the staple diet. Most restaurants and tavernas will have a 'paella day' at least once a week and our village is no different, with Friday being the day when theirs hits the tables – and they make a delicious vegetarian version, too. The latter is exceptional given the fact that the original recipe is based on fish, shellfish, chicken and rabbit and putting peas in the dish was out of the question. Paella was also traditionally served on Sundays, but only given to the male members of the family. Well, that was then, this is now. The dark-red colour of this version comes from the perla negra rice I use. The colour of this rice is not the result of some trick or other, but is down to the fact that the kernels have not been de-husked. It is the same rice that is used to make sushi. A welcome benefit is that this makes the rice much more nutritious and it contains more antioxidants, fibres and vitamin E than you will find in blueberries.

serves *4* | preparation time *35* minutes

1 litre water
2 vegetable stock cubes
300 g perla negra (black rice)
1 red onion
4 cloves of garlic
1 fennel bulb
1 red pepper
1 yellow pepper
60 ml extra virgin olive oil
1 tsp chilli powder

1 tsp ground cumin
1 tsp turmeric
240 ml dry sherry
150 g Kalamata olives
300 g artichoke hearts (from a jar/tin)
150 g cherry tomatoes or mini pomodori
300 g frozen peas
2 lemons, cut into wedges
sea salt and freshly ground black pepper
1 handful fresh parsley, finely chopped

Bring the water to the boil and add the stock cubes and the (washed) rice. Bring it back to the boil, turn down the heat, cover and leave to simmer for 25 minutes. In the meantime, chop all the vegetables: dice the onion, finely chop the garlic, chop the fennel into thin slices and do the same with the peppers. Heat the olive oil in a large shallow frying pan and fry the onion for 5 minutes. Add the garlic fry for another minute. Then add the peppers and the fennel and continue frying for another 5 minutes. Add the spices: chilli, cumin and turmeric. Fry for 1 minute, pour in the sherry and add the rice and stock and the peas. Give it a good stir, season with salt and pepper and do not stir anymore. Turn down the heat and put a lid on the pan or cover it with aluminium foil. Leave to simmer about 20 minutes, but after 10 minutes stir in the cherry tomatoes (halved), olives and the artichoke hearts (quartered). Cover again with the lid or foil. Garnish with the fresh parsley and lemon wedges before serving.

In the evening

Quinoa with
CANNELLINI BEANS
and Swiss chard

I came up with this recipe one memorable day when I had absolutely no interest in going into town to buy something for dinner but then discovered that I didn't have anything left in the cupboard either. I was faced with a choice: make something that the kids would instantly suspect as being a tad macrobiotic, or give in and join the long queues at the supermarket. It wasn't an easy choice, I'll admit, but in the end, I went with the former and decided to brave the inevitable complaints of my children. The result was a startling success.

serves *4* | preparation time *25* minutes

250 g quinoa
2 tbsp coconut oil
1 medium-sized onion, diced
2 cloves of garlic, finely chopped
large bunch of Swiss chard, leaves and stalks
  finely chopped

400 g cannellini beans (1 tin or jar), drained
3 teaspoons of fresh or dried thyme
sea salt and freshly ground black pepper
extra virgin olive oil (optional)

Wash the quinoa thoroughly in a fine mesh colander and add it to a saucepan of boiling water (2 parts water to 1 part quinoa) along with 1 teaspoon of salt. Bring back to the boil, turn down the heat, cover and leave to cook for 12–14 minutes. Check now and then to see if the white spots on the quinoa grains have disappeared and when they have, drain off the excess water, cover and set aside (if you overcook the quinoa it will get too soft). In the meantime, heat the coconut oil in a pan and fry the onion on a low heat for 5–7 minutes until soft. Add the garlic and fry for 1 more minute. Turn up the heat, add the chard and fry for a further 2–3 minutes. Add the thyme and the cannellini beans and stir-fry until the beans are hot enough. Finally, stir in the cooked quinoa and season to taste with 1 teaspoon of salt and pepper. If you think the dish is too dry, you can add a dash of extra virgin olive oil.

In the evening

FRIED SPINACH
and celeriac mash

My love for mash will probably endure forever. However, it is not that long ago that we were being told that potatoes were bad for you and that we needed to seriously cut down on carbohydrates. So, I started to experiment with other ingredients. Celeriac, for example, turned out to be a great substitute for the poor old spud! In the meantime, the hype has passed and I am eating potatoes again, as well as all the other carbs that I love – grains, pastas, bread and pizzas – but this recipe has not been forgotten. It is quite delicious and perfect for those who are looking for a low-carb alternative to potatoes.

serves *4* | preparation time *35* minutes

2½ tsp salt
1 large celeriac
50 ml (soya) cream
50 g butter, plus an extra knob (optional)
3 tbsp olive oil for frying
1 large onion, diced

2 cloves of garlic, finely chopped
300 g spinach
freshly ground black pepper
pinch of nutmeg for garnishing

Add a teaspoon of salt to a saucepan of water and bring to the boil. Peel the celeriac, chop it into chunks and cook for 15 minutes and drain when done. Mash the celeriac with the cream and the butter and season with 1½ teaspoons of salt and pepper. In the meantime, fry the onion in olive oil for about 5 minutes until soft and then add the garlic and fry for another minute. Add the spinach and cook until it has shrunk. Then add the spinach and onion mix to the mash and stir in gently. Taste to see of it needs more salt and/or pepper, garnish with a pinch of nutmeg and serve with an extra knob of butter if you like.

In the evening

Pasta
PESTO
with cherry tomatoes in white wine

'Pasta pesto' is like an old friend you can always depend on. It is also perfect for when you want to put something tasty on the table in double-quick time. However, it wasn't until I decided to add cherry tomatoes braised in white wine that I knew I really had an ace up my sleeve!

serves *4* | preparation time *25* minutes

500 g (whole wheat) spaghetti
500 g cherry tomatoes, halved
1 clove of garlic, finely chopped
3 tbsp olive oil for frying
300 ml dry white wine
1 tbsp dried thyme
sea salt and freshly ground black pepper
grated Parmesan cheese for garnish

Pesto
40 g fresh basil
40 g Parmesan cheese
1 clove of garlic, crushed
120 ml extra virgin olive oil
40 g pine nuts
½ tsp sea salt and freshly ground black pepper

Cook the spaghetti al dente according to the instructions with a teaspoon of salt. Drain and stir in a drop or two of olive oil. While the pasta is cooking, heat the olive oil, add the tomatoes and garlic and fry on a high heat for 3 minutes, keeping the tomatoes whole. Season with salt and pepper, pour in the wine and then add the thyme. Bring it to the boil, reduce the heat and leave to simmer for about 7 minutes. In the meantime, make the pesto by mixing all the ingredients together with a hand blender. Divide the spaghetti between the plates, add the tomato sauce and then the pesto. Serve topped with Parmesan cheese.

In the evening

Warm
POTATO SALAD
with mixed tomatoes

A potato salad, you might say, but this one has a twist. This salad looks fabulous thanks to the fabulous colours. It is great as a side dish, but can also be served as a main meal as it is very high in nutrients.

serves *6-8* | preparation time *40* minutes

Salad
600 g potatoes, peeled
300 g mixed tomatoes (small and large, red and yellow).
4 balls of burrata, torn into pieces
150 g Kalamata or black olives, deseeded and halved
4 tbsp capers
2 handfuls fresh basil, leaves only
1 handful chives, finely chopped
sea salt

Red wine dressing
3 tbsp red wine vinegar
1 clove of garlic, crushed
2 tsp honey
1 shallot, very finely chopped
60 ml extra virgin olive oil
1 tsp sea salt and freshly ground black pepper
2 tsp mustard
1 tbsp mayonnaise

Cook the potatoes in plenty of water with a pinch of salt for no more than 20 minutes. Drain and set aside to cool a little. In the meantime, slice the larger tomatoes and halve the smaller ones. Make the dressing by mixing all the ingredients together (in a jar with a lid). Cut the potatoes into firm slices and arrange them on a flat plate or serving dish with the tomatoes and the burrata. Sprinkle with the basil and chives before adding the capers and olives to the salad. Pour the dressing over the salad just before serving.

In the evening

SWEET STUFF

I must admit that I don't have much of a sweet tooth and am not really the best person to ask for advice when it comes to desserts. But I have managed to remember some good stuff down through the years, primarily thanks to the fact that I now have three kids, and I will try my hand at something sweet every now and then. And after the avocado cheesecake that I recently made proved to be a resounding success, I decided I did like making desserts after and duly promised my children that I would spend more time making cakes, cookies and puddings from now on – roll on book number two.

Fruit with
MASCARPONE
and dessert wine

Last year, when we had been invited by friends to dinner, we were asked if we would like to make the dessert. I have no idea why, because I'm certainly not known for my desserts. Anyway, I had to think up something to make, so we went to the nearest shop in the hope of finding some inspiration. We saw so much fresh fruit lying around that Nicholas and I decided on the spot that we would be able to make a great dessert if we combined the fruit with mascarpone, crunchy waffle biscuits, fresh mint and sweet dessert wine. Thankfully we were right and our efforts proved to be an enormous success.

serves *4* | preparation time *10* minutes

250 g mascarpone cheese
4 tbsp full-fat yoghurt
100 ml dessert wine, for example, Muscat
150 g blueberries
150 g raspberries

3 nectarines, in wedges
1 lime, in wedges
zest of 1 lime
8 crunchy waffle biscuits
1 handful fresh mint leaves, finely chopped

Mix the mascarpone cheese with the yoghurt and the dessert wine. Wash and dry the fruit and divide it between 4 plates and top off with a dollop of mascarpone (use it all up). Sprinkle with the fresh mint, the biscuit pieces and the lime zest. Add a wedge of lime and finish off with an extra dash of dessert wine. This dessert is divine.

In the evening

Grandma Kitty's
SPONGE FINGERS

When Grandma Kitty comes to visit us in Ibiza, we can always be sure of one thing: we will spend the week eating the most fabulous desserts! The pounds will be piled on, but that doesn't stop us from indulging ourselves for one week of the year. Because if there is one thing that Grandma Kitty is good at then it is making the most delicious treats. I never, ever get in her way; I like to encourage those who show some initiative...

serves *4-6* | preparation time *15* minutes

250 ml cream
125 ml lemon juice
6 tbsp agave syrup
250 g mascarpone cheese
± 15 sponge finger biscuits (depending on thickness)
1 handful fresh mint
zest of 1 lime and 1 lemon
dark chocolate shavings (optional)

First, whip the cream with 75 ml lemon juice and the agave syrup before adding in the mascarpone cheese. Arrange a layer of sponge fingers on your best platter or serving dish and sprinkle with half of the remaining lemon juice. Then spread half of the cream-mascarpone mix and repeat for the next layer. Garnish with the zest, fresh mint and the chocolate shavings if you like. Now, dig in!

In the evening

Refreshing
YOGHURT DESSERT
with peach and rich tea biscuits

Again, it was my brother who turned up trumps when he first made this dessert for us a few years ago. He probably doesn't remember it himself anymore but we certainly do! The only drawback is that it demands a little patience because it needs at least two hours in the fridge to firm up. But believe me, your patience will be rewarded, and then some.

serves *4* | preparation time *10* minutes (plus 2 hours in the fridge)

125 ml cream
3 tbsp agave syrup
250 ml full-fat yoghurt
juice of ½ lemon
6 half peaches, from tin/jar, chopped
200 g digestive biscuits, rolled into crumbs

Whip the cream with the agave syrup until stiff. Then fold in the yoghurt and the lemon juice. Spoon half of this mixture into 4 glasses, retaining the rest for the second layer. Add a layer of peach and a layer of biscuit crumbs before topping off with the second layer of yoghurt and cream. Garnish with extra peach if you like. Leave to firm up in the fridge for at least 2 hours before serving.

Avocado
CHEESECAKE

I had been planning on making a healthier variety of cheesecake for a long time. I just love cheesecakes, but the results always come back to haunt you when you stand on the scales the next day. You could probably save yourself the trouble of making it in the first place by just plastering six pounds of butter onto your hips. But that would also mean denying yourself the pleasure of eating it. So, in the end I came up with a green version using avocados. Now, there are lots of people who think that avocados make you fat too. Nonsense. Okay, maybe if you eat ten in one sitting, but one avocado a day is very good for you. They may indeed have a high fat content, but those fats are the good monounsaturated fatty acids that help keep your cholesterol levels in check. Avocado is also packed with fibre (good for the digestive system) and contains vitamins B, K and E that are good for your skin, bones and eyes, respectively. So, what could possibly be wrong with eating them.

serves *8-12* | preparation time *30* minutes (plus 2 hours in the fridge)

200 g almonds
100 g walnuts
8 dates, deseeded
200 g (wholegrain) digestive biscuits
60 ml liquid coconut oil (melted in a frying pan)
8 avocados, peeled and deseeded
60 ml lime juice, plus the zest for garnishing
5 heaped tbsp organic honey (or agave or maple syrup)

180 ml liquid coconut oil (melted in a frying pan)
flesh of 1 vanilla pod
1 tsp sea salt
2 punnets of raspberries
Extra: baking paper, baking tin approx. 25 cm in diameter

To make the base, put the almonds, walnuts, dates, biscuits and 8 tablespoons of heated coconut oil in a food processor and mix until you have achieved a fine, grainy texture. If you don't have a food processor, you can resort to a pestle and mortar and lots of good old-fashioned elbow grease. Line the cake tin with baking paper, add the biscuit mixture and press it down firmly with the back of a spoon. Then use a hand blender to combine the ingredients for the filling (avocado, lime juice, honey or syrup, 180 ml liquid coconut oil, vanilla and salt); mix until smooth. Spread the filling over the biscuit base and top off with the raspberries. Place the cheesecake in the fridge for at least 2 hours to allow it to firm up. Sprinkle with the lime zest before serving.

In the evening

Griddled
PEACHES
with blue cheese and honey vinaigrette

There is something wonderfully decadent about warm fruit and cheese. This is also a great dessert to serve when you want to make a lasting impression, despite being so easy to make.

serves *4* | preparation time *10* minutes

4 peaches, skinned, deseeded and halved (or from a tin)
1 tbsp olive oil
75 g blue cheese
4 tbsp dark honey
handful of walnuts, crushed

Heat the olive oil in a griddle pan and cook the peaches on both sides until they are nicely striped. Place two peach halves on each plate (round side down), and crumble the blue cheese on the top. Add the walnuts and 1 tablespoon of honey per plate and serve immediately.

ACKNOWLEDGMENTS

Writing and publishing this book has been a dream come true, but I could never have done it on my own. Many of the recipes were created especially for this book, but a lot of the original ideas were inspired by memories of wonderful dinners or lunches on the beach in the company of friends and family. There is a story behind every dish and therein lies the secret to cooking and eating together: that you do it for and with each other; that in the process of enjoying delicious and healthy food together you also get to create great memories that will last a lifetime!

I want to thank a lot of people without whom this book would never have become a reality. My kids, who showed great patience in putting up with a mother forever going around in an apron and issuing instructions, camera in hand, and a fridge that only ever seemed to contain 'healthy stuff'! My dear friend Nan, who came to Ibiza to lend a helping hand when I was struggling to meet the deadline; so unbelievably kind of you! Another dear friend, Sarah, who allowed me to take over her house and garden for a few days all because of the wonderful blue doors in her house that just had to go in the book! My brother, with whom I spent many hours in the kitchen trying out new recipes and who always seemed to be able to find a creative solution whenever we needed one! And not forgetting my handsome, talented husband, who managed to turn hundreds of photos, miles of text and millions of corrections into a beautiful book.

I also wish to express my gratitude to my wonderful publishers, Hans and Peter, for showing such faith in me, in us, for giving us all the room to manoeuvre we needed and for believing that the result would be worth it! Thank you! Thanks also to Sluiz, the fantastic Dutch 'feelgood' shop here on Ibiza that provided all of the fabulous, multi-coloured plates and dishes used in the photos. And, of course, Sanne at the wonderful Finca Ecologica, where we also took some amazing photographs. And last, but not least, Jennifer Arndt, who took the photos during our splendid 'grand finale lunch'.

To all my friends and family, to the beautiful island and people of Ibiza, to our beloved animals: thank you for all your help and for being there when I needed you.

Mirjam

www.SluizIbiza.com
www.JenniferArndt.com
www.HotKitchen.com

INDEX

A

agave syrup 43, 225, 227
almonds 39, 57, 229
almond milk 39, 43, 52
American blueberry pancakes 43
apple 39, 52, 133
artichokes 207, 209
asparagus 35, 117, 123, 125, 189
aubergine 101, 181
Aunty Marcel's strawberries 71
avocado 41, 51, 61, 93, 99, 117, 123, 125, 141, 160, 161, 221, 229
avocado cheesecake 229
avocado-coriander dressing 161

B

basil 27, 51, 61, 71, 101, 149, 157, 217, 219
basil pesto 162
beans 29, 33, 61, 81, 93, 99, 162, 169, 187, 211
beetroot 87
beetroot shoots 123
black bean tapenade with cumin 162
black beans 93, 162, 169, 187
black olives 73, 163, 219
blue cheese 67
blueberries 43, 57, 223
blueberry sauce 43
broad beans 29, 121, 187
broccoli 45, 65, 67, 95, 117, 155, 173, 195
brown lentils 77, 183
Brussels sprouts 121
buckwheat and chickpea flour pancakes 79

buckwheat flour 79
buffalo mozzarella 87
Burrata 61
Burrata salad with beans and fresh herbs 61

C

Caesar dressing 103, 160
Caesar salad 103
cannellini beans 81, 153, 211
capers 61, 93, 129, 161, 179, 219
carrot 95, 115
cauliflower 81, 95, 117, 183
cauliflower rice 81
chachi 41
cheddar cheese 131
chickpea flour 79
chickpeas 21, 73, 137, 162, 163, 175, 205
chilli 169
chilli pepper 93, 127, 147, 153, 159, 173
cinnamon 39, 52, 57, 157, 169
coriander 51, 61, 71, 93, 99, 107, 121, 125, 141, 153, 155, 159, 162, 163, 169, 183, 205
coriander hummus 163
courgette 55, 77, 101, 137, 141, 159, 167, 181, 193
cranberries 57
crème fraîche 95, 151, 163, 167, 169, 183
cumin 55, 137, 153, 162, 169, 183, 209
curry 183

D E

dried peppers 121

eggs 19, 25, 29, 33, 35, 41, 45, 51, 67, 73, 91, 103, 111, 123, 125, 129, 131, 137, 175
endive 81

F

fantastic egg salad 111
farmer's quinoa pie 131
farro 171
farotto 171
fennel 155, 199, 209
feta 65, 115, 127
flat leaf parsley 55, 65, 77, 85, 93, 107, 111, 115, 121, 143, 155, 160, 163, 175, 187, 197, 207
French beans 61, 117, 129, 137, 187
French onion soup from the garden 41, 139
fried eggs with broad beans 29
Fries (sweet potato) 177
Fruit with mascarpone 223

G

gazpacho 141
goat's cheese 79, 131, 171
ginger 39, 133, 137, 183, 205
glass noodles 125
golden milk 39
gorgonzola 67
Grandma Kitty's sponge fingers
granola 57
grapefruit 87
Greek yoghurt 29, 47
Greek yoghurt with griddled nectarine and pistachio nuts 47
green asparagus 123, 125, 189
green beans 137
green goddess dressing 160
green pancakes 91
green paprika 141

green salad with edamame beans and warm caper vinaigrette 129
griddled asparagus with egg and Parmesan cheese 35

H

hashbrowns with courgette and sweet potato 55
hazelnut oil 87
heirloom tomato salad 107
homemade granola 57
honey 21, 39, 107, 117, 123, 125, 129, 157, 160, 161, 163, 199, 219, 229, 231
hummus 162

J K

Japanese glass noodle salad 125
Kalamata olives 123, 209
kale 131, 155, 171
kidney beans 169

L

La Paloma salad 117
lasagne with spinach and crème fraîche 167
lentils 77, 183, 187, 193
lentil salad with raw courgette 77
lettuce 103, 123, 129
lime 27, 47, 77, 93, 103, 133, 160, 161, 171, 183, 223, 225

M

macadamia nuts 57
mango 33, 52, 117, 127
mango & strawberry ice cream 33
maple syrup 47, 57, 229

Veggie Very Much

mega-bean salad 99
Mexican salsa 162
mint 29, 33, 47, 53, 73, 87, 115, 125, 127,
    133, 179, 223, 225
mixed spring salad 123
muffins 45
mushrooms 153, 167, 175, 197
mustard dressing 160
mustard soup with orange and sweet potato 143

N

Nan's dip 95, 163
nectarines 47
noodles 125
nutritional yeast flakes 103, 205

O

oat flour 43
oat milk 43
oatmeal 39, 43, 52, 57
oatmeal pancakes 43
oats 39
oeuf cocotte with parsley pesto 25
olive tapenade 163
omelette, quinoa-stuffed 51
onion soup 139
oranges 133, 143, 161, 169
overnight oats with golden milk 39

P

padron peppers 203
paella 209
pancakes 43, 79, 91
Parmesan cheese 25, 35, 55, 61, 103, 115, 121,
    129, 131, 139, 162, 163, 167, 171, 173, 179,
    189, 201, 217

parsley 25, 55, 65, 73, 77, 85, 93, 107, 111,
    115, 121, 143, 155, 160, 163, 175, 187, 197,
    207, 209
parsley pesto 25
parsley-pesto dressing 115
parsnip 117
pasta with cherry tomatoes in white wine 217
pasta with capers and mint 179
pea and mint soup 151
peaches 227, 231
peas 115, 151, 209
pecan nuts 57
peppers 99, 121, 141, 149, 181, 203, 205
pistachio 47
pistachio nuts 57
pizza 191, 193, 195, 197
potage de vigilia 137
potato salad 219
puff pastry 67, 101

Q

quinoa 10, 21, 51, 65, 115, 131, 187, 199, 211
quinoa tart 131
quinoa-stuffed omelette 51

R

radishes 95, 123
raspberries 53, 133, 223, 229
raw beetroot with buffalo mozzarella 87
red onion 99, 131
remoulade sauce 93
ricotta 67, 101, 195, 201
risotto 189
roasted Caesar salad 103
roasted carrot salad with sourdough bread,
    young peas and parsley pesto 115
roasted peppers 149, 205
rocket 147, 193, 197

rocket soup with chilli pepper 147
romaine lettuce 103
roman cauliflower 117
rosemary 81, 133, 161
rosemary dressing 161

S

salad of endive and cannellini beans with
    cauliflower 'rice' 81
salad of parsley and red onion 85
salad of raw Brussels sprouts and broad beans
    121
salty strawberries shake with basil 27
savoury broccoli muffins 45
savoury tart 101
sesame oil 99, 125, 163
smoothies 53
soba noodles 117
soup 73, 135, 151, 159
sourdough bread 41, 115
soya dip with onions 163
sourdough bread 41, 115
soya dip with onions 163
soya dressing 125, 161
soya milk 51, 53, 91
soya sauce 125, 161, 163
Spanish mega-bean salad with avocado and
    sesame oil 99
spicy chickpea salad 73
spinach 67, 85, 91, 117, 137, 155, 167, 171,
    175, 189, 205, 215
steamed broccoli 65
strawberries 27, 33, 53, 71
strawberry shake with basil 27
stuffed sweet potato with remoulade sauce 93
sublime parsley and red onion salad 85
sweet potato 55, 93
sweet chilli sauce 125

T

tahini dressing 161
tahini paste 117
tapenade 162, 163
tarragon 107
tarts 67, 101, 131
thyme 101, 151, 171, 181, 201
tomatoes 123, 141, 149, 157, 162, 167, 175,
    181, 201, 219
tomato soup with roasted peppers 149
tomato soup with turmeric 149, 157
turmeric 39, 137, 143, 157, 183, 205, 209

V

veg with Nan's dip 95
vegetable pie 67
vinaigrette 160
vinaigrette with soya and sambal oelek 161
vinaigrettes 160

W

walnuts 57, 65, 115, 123, 229, 231
warm caper vinaigrette 129
warm salad with steamed broccoli and feta 65
water 133
watermelon with mango, feta and mint 127
white beans 99, 187
white wine 139, 151, 167, 171, 189, 217
wholemeal flour 91
wholemeal toast 29

Y

yoghurt 27, 29, 33, 47, 52, 53, 57, 93, 151,
    161, 169, 183, 223, 227

URBAN HEALTHY RECIPES

AMS 2012

VEGGIE

~VERY MUCH~

DOT COM